Developing Natural Curiosity through Project-Based Learning

Developing Natural Curiosity through Project-Based Learning is a practical guide that provides step-by-step instructions for PreK-3 teachers interested in embedding project-based learning (PBL) into their daily classroom routine. The book spells out the five steps teachers can use to create authentic PBL challenges for their learners and illustrates exactly what that looks like in an early childhood classroom. Authentic project-based learning experiences engage children in the mastery of twenty-first-century skills and state standards to empower them as learners, making an understanding of PBL vital for PreK-3 teachers everywhere.

Dayna Laur is an independent educational consultant. Dayna leads workshops on PBL, authentic learning experiences, inquiry learning, critical thinking, Advanced Placement, technology integration, 1:1 programs, and STEAM. She trains nationally, internationally, and through online support.

Jill Ackers is a school leader, instructional coach, and teacher who consults for schools and universities all over the world and virtually. She is passionate about curriculum and instruction, leadership, and program design.

Other Eye On Education Books
Available from Routledge
(www.routledge/eyeoneducation)

What Schools Don't Teach:
20 Ways to Help Students Excel in School and Life
Brad Johnson and Julie Sessions

The Fearless Classroom:
A Practical Guide to Experiential Learning Environments
Joli Barker

Less is More in Elementary School:
Strategies for Thriving in a High-Stakes Environment
Renee Rubin, Michelle Abrego, and John Sutterby

Close Reading in Elementary School:
Bringing Readers and Texts Together
Diana Sisson and Betsy Sisson

Creating a Classroom Culture That Supports the Common Core:
Teaching Questioning, Conversation Techniques, and
Other Essential Skills
Bryan Harris

Developing Natural Curiosity through Project-Based Learning

Five Strategies for the PreK-3 Classroom

Dayna Laur and Jill Ackers

Routledge
Taylor & Francis Group

NEW YORK AND LONDON

First published 2017
by Routledge
711 Third Avenue, New York, NY 10017

and by Routledge
2 Park Square, Milton Park, Abingdon, Oxon OX14 4RN

Routledge is an imprint of the Taylor & Francis Group, an informa business

© 2017 Taylor & Francis

Library of Congress Cataloguing in Publication Data
Names: Laur, Dayna, author. | Ackers, Jill, author.
Title: Developing natural curiosity through project-based learning : five strategies for the preK-3 classroom / by Dayna Laur and Jill Ackers.
Description: Milton Park, Abingdon, Oxon ; New York, NY : Routledge, 2017. | Includes bibliographical references.
Identifiers: LCCN 2016035125| ISBN 9781138694200 (hardback) | ISBN 9781138694217 (pbk.) | ISBN 9781315528410 (ebook)
Subjects: LCSH: Project method in teaching. | Early childhood education—Curricula.
Classification: LCC LB1139.35.P8 L38 2017 | DDC 372.21—dc23
LC record available at https://lccn.loc.gov/2016035125

ISBN: 978-1-138-69420-0 (hbk)
ISBN: 978-1-138-69421-7 (pbk)
ISBN: 978-1-315-52841-0 (ebk)

Typeset in Palatino
by Book Now Ltd, London

Contents

Figures

Tables

Meet the Authors

Dayna Laur is a veteran classroom teacher of nearly twenty years and is a two-time National Board Certified Teacher. She has been featured in Edutopia's "Schools that Work" video series, and as a model teacher for Authentic Learning by the National Institute for Professional Practice. She produced "Teaching Fundamentals: Project-Based Learning" with Lynda.com and currently collaborates with teachers both nationally and internationally on ways to make their classrooms authentic learning environments. Dayna has a B.A. in History from Virginia Tech, an M.Ed. in Curriculum and Instruction from the University of Pittsburgh, an M.S.Ed. in 21st Century Teaching and Learning from Wilkes University, and is currently working on her Ed.D. in Instructional Technology from Sam Houston State University. Her first book, *Authentic Learning Experiences: A Real-World Approach to PBL*, was also published with Routledge. Dayna is a wife and a mother of two girls. She loves spending time at their sporting events and riding horses with her family. You can follow her on Twitter @daylynn.

Jill Ackers has over twenty years of experience in teaching, coaching, and administration in public and private K–12 schools and in higher education. She began her career as a math teacher and later moved into technology. While earning her CCNA & MCSE certifications, she managed the school's networks and taught K–8 technology in Denver, Colorado. After relocating to Dallas, Texas, she was a founding member of a K–12 International Baccalaureate STEM school. As the IB Coordinator, her role was to strategically plan the school culture, conduct teacher evaluations, and design the professional development—leading to the school's official IB World School authorization. She later transitioned to higher education and was a part of the design team for Southern Methodist University's first urban principal Master's Degree program, a program to transform urban public schools and leaders. Upon completion of the program's design, Jill pioneered the city's first dual-language PBL elementary school and served as the Elementary Director. Jill travels extensively, both nationally and internationally, facilitating workshops for professors, school leaders, and teachers. She has a B.S. in Applied

Learning and Development and Elementary Education and a M.Ed. in School Leadership and Administration. She is currently working on her Ed.D. in Instructional Technology from Sam Houston State University. She lives with her husband, two daughters, and three dogs. Her passions include being outdoors, rescuing and fostering German Shepherds, and staying active.

1

Developing Ideas for Authentic Challenges, Projects, Learning Experiences

How do we foster a child's natural curiosities to empower them as learners?

An Introduction to Authentic Challenges, Projects, Learning Experiences

Young minds have an amazing capacity to see challenges, not as problems that can't be solved, but rather as puzzles waiting to be mastered. However, many adults approach early childhood education with an attitude of "they are too young to tackle real challenges." We know this is far from the truth as all children are born with an innate natural curiosity. As they learn how to crawl and grab at each new object or dig in the dirt and catch bugs, each experience produces new discoveries and new knowledge. This instinctive desire to learn has the potential to grow or the possibility to be squandered. Thus, it is our responsibility to foster this natural curiosity through guidance and the facilitation of what we collectively refer to in this book as authentic challenges, projects, and learning experiences.

> **Take Note**: We use the terms authentic challenges, projects, project-based learning, and learning experiences interchangeably throughout the book. We know they are all commonly used terms in education and depending on your set of circumstances, your district or school may have chosen to adopt a particular reference. We collectively think of them as open-ended, inquiry-driven approaches to education.

How do we foster a child's natural curiosities to empower them as learners? Give a child a blank piece of paper and a box of crayons and divergent learning is fostered. They have an uninhibited imagination that allows their make-believe world to take over. The colors and lines are blurred into a reality of complex and intricate scenes. Give a child a coloring book with that same box of crayons and instead, scribbles outside of the lines are the norm. Their imagination is now limited to the confines of the given picture. This simple example illustrates the beauty of crafting authentic learning experiences for learners. Young children need to have opportunities to solve real challenges. In order to have each learning experience build upon the other, we must provide them with an environment to develop their thought patterns. Our learners establish a greater understanding of the world in which they live when they are given the chance to connect their experiences in a meaningful way. If we design open-ended, real-life challenges, rather than simply scripting a craft or an activity, we then allow our children to explore and discover (Table 1.1). These explorations deepen natural curiosities, promote learner growth, and lead to endless possibilities for discovery.

TABLE 1.1 Teaching Activities versus Authentic Learning Experiences

Teaching Activities	Authentic Learning Experiences
Directions	Decisions
Constraints	Flexibility
Prompting	Initiative
Workstations	Learning Stations
Duplication	Guided Exploration
Desired Outcome	Open-ended Possibilities
End Product	Process Reflection

Teaching activities provide learners with opportunities to identify and apply content standards. Teacher prompting and workstations supply time to practice skills and reinforce content already taught. Specifically, workstations are designed to allow learners, independently or in small groups, to explore given instructional materials without the assistance of their teacher. This exploration is important to support a solid foundation of essential content. However, when exploration is limited to those materials and rarely extends beyond those materials, we only see the refinement of basic skills.

A learning station, in contrast, is where academic content occurs as a natural part of the authentic learning experience. This is where learners progress toward finding solutions to a given challenge, issue, or problem. The material for interaction and inquiry is provided prior to any teaching that occurs. This allows for guided exploration as learners work collaboratively to assume an active role in the discovery process, in both a reflective and communicative capacity. Here, learners begin to analyze, summarize, and paraphrase. This provides us with a look into their selected inquiry paths. It means you will not teach your learners what they need to know before the authentic project starts. Rather, children choose their learning path based on what they want to know about the challenge. Once an in-depth investigation has begun, you determine the needed levels of scaffolding, established by the interactions between learner and teacher chosen materials. This moves our learners to the next phase of the authentic project.

Young children are frequently given directions on how to complete something. These directions may be as simple as how to tie a shoe, hold a pencil, spell a word, or play a game. Directions are useful for many basic activities. However, to develop learners who are problem-solvers and eagerly accept new challenges requires them to become flexible in their approach to learning. They must be the decision-makers. This means that we must limit the number of constraints that are placed on our learners and provide them with opportunities for autonomy. We want to foster their ability to take initiatives in their own learning, so it is necessary to help learners see the world in which they live with new perspective. This is a world full of possibilities.

Teaching activities hold a valuable place in our daily instructional practice. They are the basic scaffolds our learners need to transition from the recall of a simple definition or fact to the application of their academic language in context. Learners who articulate the content and skills of your standards use academic language to demonstrate what they know and are able to do. This application of academic language is imperative for them to understand the more complex nature of the classroom. It is in contrast to the conversational tone of social settings (see Figure 1.1). However, teaching activities are intended to have predetermined, desired outcomes. These outcomes provide evidence of understanding at the lower levels of Bloom's Taxonomy, but generally constrain the approach by the learner (see Table 1.2). Authentic projects, in comparison, are designed to help learners climb up the ladder to higher levels of thinking. This challenges them to evaluate their inferences and draw more accurate conclusions. This, in turn, provides a better assessment of what learners know and are able to do with their knowledge.

We are fortunate to work with children whose young minds are still receptive to open-ended possibilities and don't beg for the "one right answer." We must be careful to ensure an allowance for guided exploration without pushing our own preconceived ideas about a desired outcome onto these eager minds. As facilitators, we must think primarily about the authentic learning experience as a process, rather than focus solely on the end product. The process reflection that takes place during an authentic project provides our learners with the opportunity to gain new levels of independence and autonomy, and to take ownership of their experiences. Through these experiences, our learners become more confident and are eager for another adventure as new and exciting challenges are presented (see Table 1.3).

Teaching and learning activities support our children in their quest to manipulate information as they apply and evaluate their inferences to a big idea or project challenge. The heart of an authentic learning experience comes from the melding of best instructional practices. While a teaching activity is generally a stand-alone experience, an authentic task is an interconnected series of activities. The use of teaching tasks and activities as scaffolds elevate a child's ability to make connections between their learning and the activity. The sum of the activities, in support of a greater authentic project, pushes our learners to extend their thinking. This is the goal of the inquiry process. Learners engage with

Figure 1.1 Examples of Academic Language

Possible Teacher Questions
<ul><li>How can we **predict** the ways in which our products will address the challenge?</li><li>How can we **summarize** what we've **discovered**?</li><li>What are the **consequences** of our actions?</li><li>**If** we do X, **then** what happens to Y?</li><li>If we **present** it this way, will they **understand** that?</li></ul>

TABLE 1.2 Questions to Support the Revised Bloom's Taxonomy

Bloom's Taxonomy	Question
Creating	How would you make better ...? Can you put together a _____ to ...? Can you create new and different ways for ...? In what ways could you solve ...? If you had access to anything you needed, how would you fix ...? Why don't you come up with your own way to ...? Can you construct a _____ to ...?
Evaluating	Is there a better way to ...? Can you tell me why you think we need to do this ...? What changes to _____ would you make? How well does _____ work? What are some things that will happen after ...? What are the good and bad things related to ...? What are some other ways of looking at ...?
Analyzing	How is _____ similar to _____? What are some other ideas ...? Why did these changes happen to ...? Why doesn't the _____ work well? Can you tell the difference between ...? What were some of the reasons why ...? What made the biggest difference in ...?
Applying	In what other ways can you use ...? If you did _____ what would happen to ...? What questions did you think of as you ...? What would be the outcome if ...? Can you develop a new set of directions about ...? How can you support your answers with examples from ...? How would you group ...?
Understanding	Can you explain why ...? Can you retell in your own words ...? How would you demonstrate ...? What could have happened next ...? What about this person is ...? Can you compare this to another experience ...? How can you illustrate ...?
Remembering	What happened before and after ...? How did ...? Who did ...? Can you list ...? What is the definition of ...? When did _____ happen? How did the story end with ...?

TABLE 1.3 Teaching Activities versus Authentic Tasks

Teaching Activities	Authentic Tasks
Experiments	Product Research and Development
Coloring Pages	Authentic Drawings and Mockups
Math Worksheets	2-D Prototype and 3-D Models
Paragraph or Essay	Proposal or Brief
Video	Playwright or A Pilot TV show

the authentic challenge, ask questions based on wonderings, and begin to organize prior knowledge supported by the teaching activities in which new information has been presented.

Even our youngest learners are subjected to the testing phenomena. While most states don't push standardized testing until third grade, as learners begin to read, they take tests such as the DIBELS, DRA, NWEA MAP, IOWA, TOPEL, and even Logramos for Spanish speakers. Thus, at a young age, our learners already associate education with a graded score. Contrary to this, process reflection creates a space in which our learners grow as individuals. Rather than the requirement of a once and done experience, our learners ponder their actions and the results of those actions. From this, they make informed decisions about future resolutions. However, since we know many older learners, and even adults, have trouble reflecting on their learning, this must be a guided process for our younger learners. We ask questions of our learners. We facilitate their inquiry experience, so they are not satisfied with their one-word answers. We ask for explanations of their thinking process. Who, what, when, why, and how are all key components to this line of questioning and the line of questioning is be continuous. The deeper the questions we ask of our learner, the deeper the process reflection that takes place with him or her. When we allow and model the inquiry process through questioning, we not only support teaching and learning but we honor our young learners and their curious state of mind.

Design with Community Partnerships in Mind

Traditional projects don't take a lot of time to design, but authentic learning experiences take intentional and explicit development to ensure our learners are empowered to dig deeper into the learning process. When we design our authentic projects, we begin with the basics—standards, critical thinking, and cooperation. If these three are aligned then creativity and problem-solving result.

Let's begin with possible ideas for our design starting point. We want to focus on what is real and connected to the lives of our learners. This is paramount at this juncture in the planning phase of our authentic learning experience. It is also important to develop an open-ended challenge for our learners to tackle.

This open-ended problem is intended to facilitate the connection between the challenge and the relevancy of the challenge to our learners' everyday experiences. Relevancy is critical. However, at this age, it is limited to the world that surrounds the daily life of each learner, unless we extend their reach and connect their daily life to new experiences. This, in turn, makes that new experience a relevant one. Thus, it is imperative to make the relevancy of the challenge one that is both present and personal for our learners. Community partnerships in an authentic learning experience promote this relevancy. "My Community" is a great place to start. We think about the key attractions our community has to offer. Do we have a local park, zoo, food bank, or theatre? Perhaps we have community members with whom our learners could connect. Take a look at Table 1.4 for additional inspiration on community-based project ideas.

It is important to note that increasing the size of the community for kids at this age may become overwhelming. For our youngest children, the backyard is something with which they are familiar, but a trip to the city 30 minutes away may be too much for them to immediately tackle. However, the increased frequency of opportunities to interact with our greater community will result in deeper connections between our learners and our community. This allows us to provide more opportunities to expand our community focus.

The key is to use these community partnerships to foster the natural curiosity present in our learners. We don't want to merely use these community assets to tell them information about their community and about the roles of members of the community. We use these places and people as true assets by having them assist in the learning process, as our learners uncover questions and develop solutions to the challenges posed. We may even want to work in tandem with these community partnerships in developing the authentic project. What challenges can they bring to the classroom to make your curriculum more authentic and relevant?

Community partnerships are also a great way to make learning come alive and to ensure that the learning doesn't end once the school day is

TABLE 1.4 Community-Based Project Ideas

Community Attraction	Project Idea
Theatre	Write a community-based play Create a marionette performance
Park	Sponsor a park conservation event Design a plan to make children more active by using the park in new ways
Food Bank	Develop kid-generated cookbooks to give away at the food bank Senior Box Letters—develop a pen pal program with seniors citizens who receive box lunches from the local food banks
Zoo	Create a campaign to improve the viewing spaces outside of the animal habitats from a 3–4 foot perspective Offer a redesign of various exhibits to make them more child friendly
Botanical Gardens	Design an interactive exhibit where young visitors can play to learn about the parts of a plant Create a walking tour, as they learn about the life cycles of plants and insects, that highlights the best photographic spaces for families with little kids
Fire House	Design a persuasive video to convince your family why you need a survival kit and develop the emergency evacuation plan for your home Plan a natural disaster assembly at your school to help to update the school's emergency plans
Animal Shelter	Partner with a local shelter to devise a plan to increase the number of animals adopted Design a plan to help reduce the number of animals dropped off at the shelter
Library	Develop a mini-lending library house for the neighborhood Plan an "open-mic" night for original short story readings

complete. A child may leave school for a long weekend and take a trip to the local park. As we utilize the community connection in the classroom, the child is now able to look at the park as more than just a place to play, but as a place to learn. They may begin an analysis of playground equipment in simple mathematical practice. They may find insects and ask inquiry questions about life cycles. They may also think about ways to problem solve how to get kids to share the slide in a more equitable way. In short, community partnerships promote lifelong learning practices and bring meaning and relevance to the development of critical and emotional thinking.

The Emotional, Social, and Critical Thinking Ecosystem

Once our learners connect how authentic learning is relevant to their daily experiences, we support ways in which thinking is made visible throughout the learning process. First, we begin with the cultivation of an environment grounded in emotional, social, and critical thinking (Figure 1.2). Without these connections, learners will not necessarily see the value in the content they are asked to tackle. This includes the emergent reading and writing skills they are developing as they mature between Pre-K to third grade.

Emotional thinking is related to how a learner's judgment is applied to situations. Do we make the decision to cross the road, alone, without looking both ways? Or, do we cross that same road while an adult is telling us it is okay to do so? At this age and stage, children are very reactive. Thus, the design of an authentic learning experience that promotes relevance to the world in which they live not only encourages a deeper understanding of the content, but also aids them in the development of the emotional skills necessary to navigate their world. These learning experiences also provide opportunities to engage in social settings that stimulate the growth of emotional intelligence and the skills related to it. We boost a child's emotional intelligence when we provide them with multiple occasions to work with others and in various groupings. These moments allow our learners to identify feelings and build empathy.

Social thinking aids in a child's abilities to manage group interactions and mitigate their responses to those interactions in developmentally appropriate ways. Learners begin to recognize the feelings and emotions of others, thereby developing their own negotiating and compromising skills. These social and emotional responses go hand in hand in everyday interactions, which include problem-solving and responsible decision-making. It is through authentic learning experiences and cultivated opportunities to engage in challenging projects that we allow learners the space to build and develop these skills. The more we expose

Figure 1.2 The Three Kinds of Thinking in the Classroom Ecosystem

Emotional Thinking	Social Thinking	Critical Thinking
How a learner's judgment is applied to situations	The ability to manage group interactions and mitigate their responses to those interactions	One's ability to ask, analyze, and use inferences to draw conclusions and make judgment calls

our learners to authentic challenges, the greater the increase in frequency of their appropriate social interactions. If they do not learn, early on, to navigate the developmentally appropriate, yet complex challenging situations on their own, then they are not set up for success for larger, more intricate social issues. If we deliberately include the social and emotional development in the experience, we connect the value of their feelings to their work and engage them in the process of learning how to qualify their emotions.

We know that kids, no matter what age, value examining their own thinking. Even at a young age, they have started to determine what is important and useful in their lives. Critical thinking revolves around one's ability to ask, analyze, and use inferences to draw conclusions and make judgment calls about the simplest task to the most complex task. Critical thinking, at the highest level, requires learners to create new content. Therefore, we must provide rich problem-solving opportunities to let children experience how to persevere and feel resilience through the judgment-making process, as they formulate solutions in clear and relevant ways. This problem-solving exposes our learners to the value of using the content to make the right decision for a posed challenge. In authentic projects, we can now aid them in making appropriate judgments related to their thinking during lessons and activities that are embedded in the project.

When our learners feel their decisions add merit to the challenge posed, they begin to take ownership of the learning process. That ownership promotes risk-taking. However, when authentic challenges are grounded in the standards, our learners use the standards as their content to draw academically sound inferences and conclusions. Thus, the risk-taking is rooted in an emotionally and socially safe environment. This is the link between high quality, authentic project design and learner acquisition of content knowledge through the process of critical thinking.

As early childhood educators, we realize our classroom environment is really an intricate ecosystem where all the parts and components work together. Authentic learning experiences support social and emotional development, foster critical thinking, and build confidence in young readers and writers. The process of any authentic challenge goes through five distinct stages where our learners seek an answer or solution. As teachers we plan lessons and projects based on these stages in order to meet our standards and we assess our children as they improve their skills, over time. We watch and observe them at each stage while they work through the standards and master more complex tasks to show an understanding of the content.

Five Teacher Strategies and Five Learner Stages

In Chapters 2 through 6, we explore five specific strategies to support your journey into the creation and planning of authentic project-based learning (PBL) experiences (Figure 1.3). We collectively identified these strategies to deepen and support the continual development of our learners' natural curiosity. We have developed the Five Stages to Finding a Solution during the project process to ensure that your planning supports your kids in their quest to uncover new ideas. These five stages are a way for you to chart the inquiry process of your learners. As you read each chapter, take the opportunity to begin your own planning of a project. We encourage you to refine and reflect on your current classroom pedagogy through the use of the tools and resources provided.

Throughout the book, we have aligned our Five Stages to Finding a Solution to key questions that help you understand each stage (Table 1.5). This will help you to connect each stage to your own classroom. These are questions we want you to ponder as you explore each chapter, strategy,

Figure 1.3 Five Strategies to Develop Natural Curiosity

| Strategy One: Map Standards to the Project Challenge |
| Strategy Two: Build Classroom Community |
| Strategy Three: Make Reading and Writing Authentic |
| Strategy Four: Maximize Formative Assessments |
| Strategy Five: Activate Intrinsic Motivation |

TABLE 1.5 Guiding Questions

Stages to Finding a Solution	Question
Stage 1: Authentic Challenge and Purpose	How do we know if our kids understand the challenge and why they are doing it?
Stage 2: Information and Prototyping	How do we know if our kids have created a viable prototype?
Stage 3: Perspective and Point of View	How do we know if our kids have thought about different ideas?
Stage 4: Actions and Consequences	How do we know if our kids have moved beyond their initial beliefs?
Stage 5: Considerations and Conclusions	How do we know if our kids have reached the best possible solution for their audience?

and the tools we provide to support each stage. They are the key questions that you want to have in front of you as you plan any future authentic project-based learning experience. We encourage you to use Appendix 2 as a pullout resource that you keep handy during your planning.

Every problem-solver, engineer, architect, and entrepreneur goes through stages as they work toward finding an answer to a question or as they develop a solution to a challenge. The same holds true for the learners in our classrooms. They go through these same stages as they find solutions to authentic projects. Our learners demonstrate what they know through the lessons and activities we design. We arm them with various strategies to face challenges with varied perspectives and to draw conclusions. In a project challenge, we teach our learners to use problem-solving methods and strategies to find solutions. This shifts our instructional design so it is critical thinking centered rather than lesson focused.

We now intend to arm you with strategies that are essential to instructional design. This intrinsically fosters the problem-solving process in your own classroom. As you read through the remainder of this book, you will continue to discover ways to expand your authentic ecosystem from an educator, learner, and community perspective. What are your next steps? Reflect here, before you move onto the following chapter, to uncover the tools to help you foster a child's natural curiosity and empower them as learners.

Where are You? What are You Thinking? How do You Feel?		
Take Action	**Seek Community**	**Think Aloud**
Choose two or three community resources with whom you could connect and build a relationship. Determine the ways in which your content and standards relate to these resources.	Choose an idea to share with a teaching partner and solicit feedback. Be sure to discuss the reasons for choosing the idea and its connection to building more authentic projects in your classroom.	How has the reading of this chapter changed my thinking as a designer of authentic learning experiences? What important details am I highlighting? What can I immediately implement?

2

Strategy One: Map Standards to the Project Challenge

How do I create an authentic project challenge for my classroom that meets my standards?

We know that all children come to us with varying levels of ability. At this age, it is not uncommon to have learners reading well above grade level and those who are still struggling with phonetic sounds. We may even have this large array of learners in the same classroom. Thus, to approach each challenge at the appropriate level of Bloom's Taxonomy (Table1.2) is imperative for our learners, so that we may push their current thinking ability to the next level. High quality authentic project design results in creative, relevant outcomes. This is vetted by our learner's ability to move through each of the levels of the revised Bloom's Taxonomy. However, we know that starting at the highest levels of Bloom's may be too much to ask of our learners. They need to have support and scaffolding through this process. Thus, while some may be ready, we can't expect all our learners to enter into an authentic learning experience at the level of application or evaluation. Strategy One is all about ensuring our learners use the standards as a way to exhibit their thinking from the lowest to the highest levels as they find answers to authentic challenges.

> **Take Note:** Write the challenge statement or question at the creating level of Bloom's Taxonomy using creation referenced verbs such as design, build, create, develop, plan, or construct. This is what helps our learners through the first stage of Finding a Solution.

How do I create an authentic project challenge for my classroom that meets my standards? In a traditional lesson or unit, we start at the bottom of revised Bloom's with several, or in some cases, all of our learners. In fact, the amount of time spent in each level may differ for every learner and this time may vary for each project. In any case, it is important to remember that our approach to teaching authentic projects begins with our learner as the end in mind, rather than simply the standards as the end goal. Our standards become a reflection of the learning by bringing more meaning, relevance, and consequently, more mastery. Our learners are also guided to reach the highest level of revised Bloom's Taxonomy: the level of creating. Therefore, we recommend writing your authentic challenge starting with the highest level. The highest level of revised Bloom's, creating, is where we are most able to foster the natural curiosity of our learners. The lowest levels of the revised Bloom's may prompt the inquiry of asking new questions. However, unless we push our learners to find the answers to their questions and find new solutions to challenges, their curiosity will begin to weaken and eventually fade over time (Table 2.1).

We have talked a lot about pushing our learners to the space in which they are creating to solve challenges. Our authentic learning experiences take shape when we write these high level questions. We've provided you with several examples in Chapter 1. In fact, you may have noticed that the start of each of our chapters gives you your own creation level question to answer. While we provide you with information to support you in your own quest to find your personal solutions, we also want you to take the tools we discuss and apply them in your individual journey.

If you haven't already noticed a pattern for writing these open-ended challenges, let's take a moment to break it down.

1   Start the question by making it personal. "How can I ..." or "How can we ..." are two of our favorite challenge starters. This creates buy-in for our learners and provides a more relevant context.
2   Make the question actionable. Ask your learners to do something new in the challenge. Use those creation level verbs we've mentioned before.

TABLE 2.1 Find a Solution through Bloom's

How Kids Go through Stages to Find a Solution		
Learners Think through the Stages of Finding a Solution	**Teachers Design and Plan through the Revised Bloom's Taxonomy**	
Stage 1: Authentic Challenge and Purpose How do we know if our kids understand the challenge and why they are doing it?	Understanding	
Stage 2: Information and Prototyping How do we know if our kids have created a viable prototype?	Applying	
Stage 3: Perspective and Point of View How do we know if our kids have thought about different ideas?	Analyzing	Remembering is spiraled throughout the project
Stage 4: Actions and Consequences How do we know if our kids have moved beyond their initial beliefs?	Evaluating	
Stage 5: Considerations and Conclusions How do we know if our kids have reached the best possible solution for their audience?	Creating	

3 Don't create a question that merely asks for a yes or no answer. This doesn't leave enough room for inquiry for our kids. Think about the types of questions you ponder when you notice a problem exists and you would like to see it solved.

4 Be sure that there isn't one right answer to your challenge. If you anticipate receiving final products that all look the same, go back and do some revision. While we want to meet your standards through the question, we don't want to squander the natural curiosity of our learners.

Take a quick break from reading and test yourself on writing open-ended challenges. We have provided a kindergarten example in Table 2.2 to help scaffold this process for you. Then go back to Table 1.4 in Chapter 1 and write a possible question for the challenges that we've listed. We will hold you to your honor on not peeking, but Appendix 3 has the possible answers. Check them out after you've given this a go.

TABLE 2.2 Questions through Bloom's Taxonomy

Bloom's Taxonomy	Question
Creating	How can we develop a machine from recycled materials that moves objects?
Evaluating	Does my Rube Goldberg machine show my understanding of force, motion, and the engineering design process to my intended audience members?
Analyzing	How will my design ideas change if I increase the number of pushes and pulls?
Applying	Based on my inferences, am I applying enough force to create motion with my marble?
Understanding	Have I selected the right information to begin designing my first machine prototype?
Remembering	What important information do I need to know to begin working on my challenge?

Real-world challenges bring content to life and make the standards relevant to a young learner. Therefore, the design of an authentic learning experience allows our learners to make connections to the content, while mastering required social, emotional, and academic standards. While the real-world context may be what inspires an idea for a challenge, without the standards, the project is simply an add-on to the curriculum. This is where the design process often falls short, long before the implementation even begins. Thus, choosing appropriate content and skills, to be addressed during the project process, is the first step in designing an effective authentic learning experience that meets your standards.

Choose Appropriate Content and Skills

It is easy to pick a theme or a unit of study that we enjoy teaching. Topics such as dinosaurs, weather, ecosystems, cultural and geographic systems, and many others are ones that quickly come to mind. We can think of numerous activities we may want our learners to complete and favorite lessons that have served us well over the years. However, shifting our focus to authentic and relevant content that supports the standards to be addressed aids our learners in their quest to understand their world around them (Figure 2.1).

Figure 2.1 Two Ways to Map Your Standards

Authentic Challenge ... Standards	Standards ... Authentic Challenge
What authentic challenges exist in my community?	What are my standards that lend themselves to an authentic challenge?

You may find that you prefer to start with the standards when it comes to the design of your authentic learning experience. This is a great first step and we encourage you to do this. It aids in becoming more familiar with the standards. However, you may be a big idea person and be partial to start with a project concept before moving to the standards. We will explore both starting points as possibilities, but begin our in-depth look at design by choosing the standards first.

Regardless of your grade level, take a look at your standards and begin to brainstorm authentic challenges or identify real-world connections that emerge from the standards. You do not have to start with an authentic challenge that impacts the entire local community. There are many examples of authentic challenges right in your school building that are great points of entry. In fact, this may be more comfortable for your learners. Additionally, the art of designing authentic instruction is connected to your own comfort level. It is better to design a quality challenge that directly impacts your immediate world, one with which you are intimately familiar.

For Pre-K and kindergarten, the art of designing instruction that is play-based, while still open-ended and cognitively demanding, must involve a process that includes recognizing school and state standards. This is to assist you in the identification and definition of the overall big picture of the challenge. For first and second grades, and especially third grade, play transfers to more of an inquiry-based process. It is within these grade levels that children begin to take on more responsibility for their own learning. Table 2.3 provides you with an example of a challenge at each grade level.

Here's a detailed approach we have found helps us to initiate the design of authentic learning experiences, while supporting the innate curiosity of our learners. First, choose several standards on which to focus. For example, pick three to four science standards or work with the already pre-selected, grade-level standards for a science unit. Next, circle the verbs in the standards that are those most connected to the big ideas. Keep in mind that you do not need to circle each verb, but only the verbs that support the big ideas for our project development.

Then use this list to narrow down big ideas and hone in on a product for the idea. This product becomes the tangible piece that represents how our learners answer or address the challenge.

TABLE 2.3 Standards and Possible Challenges

Standard	Possible Authentic Challenge
(Pre-K Guideline) IV.B.1 Child independently uses letters or symbols to make words or parts of words.	Curate the school like a museum and develop an art showcase through the mastery of the five basic elements of art. Invite the community to tour the exhibit.
K.CC.A.2 Count forward beginning from a given number within the known sequence (instead of having to begin at 1). K.CC.B4 Understand the relationship between numbers and quantities; connect counting to cardinality.	Redesign the idea of foursquare courts into ten frame courts. Have teams create a game, write the rules, and paint the ten frame courts on the school playground.
RI.1.3 Describe the connection between two individuals, events, ideas, or pieces of information in a text.	Have small groups of learners choose a community or family member to honor by recording them as they tell their personal story. Within your school, or as a connection with other schools from around the country, map the patterns of the stories to identify common links. Create a display of the stories and the comparisons within the school or at a community location like the local library.
K-2-ETS1-1 Ask questions, make observations, and gather information about a situation people want to change to define a simple problem that can be solved through the development of a new or improved object or tool.	Craft a plan to make your school become more sustainable and present it to the administration. Examples include: How can the school save on energy costs during the winter? How can the school's food waste be used to improve the school grounds? How can we build homegrown hay bale gardens so we can eat our own food?
W.3.1 Write opinion pieces in which they introduce the topic or book they are writing about, state an opinion, and create an organizational structure that lists reasons. Provide reasons that support the opinion. Provide a concluding statement or section.	Draft a proposal to save (or increase funding for) the art or music program for the school and submit the proposals to the school board.

Consider the following scenario:

Your principal or instructional coach walks in the room and asks "What challenges are you thinking about using to create your next authentic learning experience? What standards are you interested in using for your challenge?" You explain that you want to include informational texts and the force and motion Next Gen Science Standards. (See the full text of standards in the Rube Goldberg example in Figure 2.2.) You start to brainstorm possible events, people, and places that would allow your learners to demonstrate their understanding of force and motion. You and your coach have circled analyze, plan, and conduct as possible verbs to connect their work to a publically presented final product. You've decided not to include the verbs ask, answer, and describe, as these will support your big idea, but don't get to the heart of the challenge. Next, you and your coach focus on how to write the challenge for your project. For this, you refer back to your revised Bloom's list of verbs and concentrate on the creation level. You consider the question, "What could my learners construct that highlights their engineering skills and their mastery of the chosen standards?" Together, you look at the next four weeks of the school's calendar to seek out opportunities for your children to present their learning. The school has a parent information session for preschool parents whose children will be attending kindergarten next year. You decide this is the perfect venue for your learners to showcase their designs and highlight for incoming parents the emphasis placed on critical thinking skills in your program. You settle on the following challenge: "How can we develop a machine from recycled materials that moves objects?"

Standards to Explore

K-PS2-1. Plan and conduct an investigation to compare the effects of different strengths or different directions of pushes and pulls on the motion of an object.

K-PS2-2. Analyze data to determine if a design solution works as intended to change the speed or direction of an object with a push or a pull.

SL.K.3. Ask and answer questions in order to seek help, get information, or clarify something that is not understood. (K-PS2-2 alignment)

K.MD.A.1. Describe measurable attributes of objects, such as length or weight. Describe several measurable attributes of a single object. (K-PS2-1 alignment)

Using the given coaching scenario, let's reflect on the process of how to map the standards. Look at the overall challenge and visualize how the teacher thought about ways her learners could publicly showcase their thinking. As you design your own authentic challenge, think about the ways in which your learners' final product will meet the following goals:

1   **Relevance**: It is relevant to the real world, as it connects to the world in which your learners live.

This real world may be your school, local, state, national, or even global community. It might even be a virtual connection. These authentic challenges have multiple interpretations for final products. This real-world aspect encourages our learners to see that no two final products are the same. We want to push our learners toward a space of innovation. By providing a real-world connection, we lessen the possibility that all the products will look the same or similar. Thus, innovation stems from the need to create a relevant product or solution that fits the needs of the community.

2   **Products**: Products are designed for use beyond the classroom and for an audience outside of the teachers and classmates.

In Dayna's first book, *Authentic Learning Experiences: A Real-World Approach to Project-Based Learning*, Chapter 3 discussed, in detail, the need to create a challenge that relates to either a community or career connection. In doing so, we provide our learners with concrete experiences that help them build their understanding of the world around them. When our learners make those connections they become more adept at managing their own behavior and thought patterns. This process of reflection helps our learners to improve their academic and cooperative skills to work toward creating a high quality product. These high quality products are then ready to share with experts.

3   **Experts**: The final products are presented to authentic experts throughout the process and also a relevant audience at the end.

We may be the educational experts in the classroom, but we can't be expected to be an expert in all topics. Thus, when we utilize our community to furnish resources and expert feedback, in person and virtually, we create multiple advantages. This includes an outside perspective on the work that our learners complete. However, we can also tap into grade level experts to elicit "in house" feedback. Fifth graders provide thoughtful feedback to second graders and offer suggestions for improvement, before the prototypes are ready for subject matter experts to review. With experts, our learners must present their work and use academic language to justify their product designs. The feedback then gives us the opportunity to assess content understanding as our learners absorb expert feedback and make design changes. Additionally, these experts may serve in the capacity of providing an equally authentic audience at the conclusion of the project.

As seen in the example in Figure 2.2, we are not limited to a single subject approach to our authentic project design. In this example we drew on standards from science, math, literacy, and writing. The next step in truly moving toward an authentic model with your curriculum is to seek out and find interdisciplinary connections. Just as we know that the world outside of the classroom does not function in single subject silos, neither should we expect our learners to be limited to the exposure of just one content area at a time.

Some content areas naturally align. Science and math are frequently compatible partners, as math is deeply embedded in much of the scientific process. However, this is also the perfect time to enlist the help of our specials teachers. Art, music, and even physical education are easily integrated into an authentic project. One such first grade example may have our learners work toward designing a new or redesigning an existing playground space for the school. Measurement and geometry easily factor into this project design. Science is addressed as animal habitats may be disturbed. Literacy and writing are also incorporated with ease through the reading of books such as *The Playground Problem* (Margaret McNamara) or *My Dream Playground* (Becker) and the writing of a proposal to build the playground designed by your learners. This challenge also extends to incorporate components of healthy exercise and the development of an exercise routine, which is lead by the physical education teacher.

If you want to start with a project idea and match to the standards, this is the section for you. While we know that we can start with our standards and develop an idea from them, we may decide to first look at what is available in our community. Sometimes, we may be going about our day, reading the newspaper, or catching up on the latest gossip on social media, when we are inspired by what we see, read, or hear. Since we are the experts in our classroom and know our content and standards inside and out, we readily see these connections. For example, a news broadcast exposes the latest information on the decreased usage and subsequent decrease in funding for our local library. This may spark an idea for an authentic challenge that would have our third

Figure 2.2 Authentic Kindergarten Challenge using Science, Math, Literacy, and Writing

---

Rube Goldberg Machine

How can we develop a machine from recycled materials that moves objects?

Authentic Challenge Presented to our Learners

You will create a machine that moves a bug-filled marble from one space to another. You will develop one prototype and use feedback to improve your prototype throughout the project. During the design process, engineers and engineering students from the local university will give you feedback on your designs. At the end of the project, in groups, you will present your machines to parents and the engineers at the Parent Open House for Kindergarten Round-up. Your machines will showcase the type of learning that happens in our school, when prospective parents of preschoolers are in attendance.

Next Generation Science Standards Addressed

K-PS2-1. Plan and conduct an investigation to compare the effects of different strengths or different directions of pushes and pulls on the motion of an object. [Clarification Statement: Examples of pushes or pulls could include a string attached to an object being pulled, a person pushing an object, a person stopping a rolling ball, and two objects colliding and pushing on each other.] [Assessment Boundary: Assessment is limited to different relative strengths or different directions, but not both at the same time. Assessment does not include non-contact pushes or pulls such as those produced by magnets.]

K-PS2-2. Analyze data to determine if a design solution works as intended to change the speed or direction of an object with a push or a pull.* [Clarification Statement: Examples of problems requiring a solution could include having a marble or other object move a certain distance, follow a particular path, and knock down other objects. Examples of solutions could include tools such as a ramp to increase the speed of the object and a structure that would cause an object such as a marble or ball to turn.] [Assessment Boundary: Assessment does not include friction as a mechanism for change in speed.]

*The Next Gen Science Standards are mapped to the Common Core State Standards below.

CCSS ELA/Literacy Standards Addressed

RI.K.1. With prompting and support, ask and answer questions about key details in a text. (K-PS2-2)

RI.K.3. With prompting and support, describe the connection between two individuals, events, ideas, or pieces of information in a text. (K-PS2-2)

W.K.7. Participate in shared research and writing projects (e.g. explore a number of books by a favorite author and express opinions about them). (K-PS2-1)

SL.K.3. Ask and answer questions in order to seek help, get information, or clarify something that is not understood. (K-PS2-2)

CCSS Mathematics Standards to be Addressed

Mathematical Practice. 2. Reason abstractly and quantitatively. (K-PS2-1)

K.MD.A.1. Describe measurable attributes of objects, such as length or weight. Describe several measurable attributes of a single object. (K-PS2-1)

K.MD.A.2. Directly compare two objects with a measurable attribute in common, to see which object has "more of"/"less of" the attribute, and describe the difference. (K-PS2-1)

graders develop a plan to increase both the funding and patronage for the library. The project could easily tie in with standards related to literacy, writing, and math. We might even decide to have our children work on speaking and listening standards by performing an oral reading of stories they publish, which could then be presented to the library for use in the general collection. All authentic challenges can emanate from standards by simply looking for connections to our everyday life.

In some instances, we may be inspired by our learners' questions and ideas. However, we must be willing to stray from already determined plans and lessons if we want this to work. For example, you have a group of children that come in from recess, with their shoes full of mud, after several days of constant rain. You overhear complaints from the girls and the boys are filthier than you'd like. One little girl asks how long it will take for the mud to dry up. Another asks why the grass doesn't grow in that area. From these two simple questions, you have an authentic learning experience in the making. "How can we create a playground that is less muddy after a rainstorm?" If we allow ourselves to be open to the possibilities that may exist within the inquiring minds of our learners, amazing authentic challenges will emerge. It is up to us to then make the connection to our standards.

Another option is to start with our standards and work backward through a design process. This is the point at which we may have to dig a little deeper. Our standards, as they are written, may not overtly exhibit the real-world connections that we would like to make. We use the English Language Arts and Math Common Core State Standards and Next Generation Science Standards to illustrate this point (Figure 2.3).

There is no one right answer for the required number of standards to include in our authentic projects. Some advise that you only choose one or two and really focus on them as your "power standards." In our experience, all authentic challenges are anchored in literacy. Therefore, reading, writing, speaking, and listening standards are the foundation of any social studies or science authentic challenge. By only using one or two standards, the depth of the challenge is limited and the amount of time you devote to the work is too extensive. We hear over and over, "how can I cover all of my standards using project-based learning?" You

Figure 2.3 ELA and Math CCSS and NextGen Science Standards

Standard 1

CCSS.ELA-LITERACY.RL.K.1. With prompting and support, ask and answer questions about key details in a text.

Standard 2

CCSS.ELA-LITERACY.RI.K.2. With prompting and support, identify the main topic and retell key details of a text.

Standard 3

CCSS.ELA-LITERACY.RI.K.3. With prompting and support, describe the connection between two individuals, events, ideas, or pieces of information in a text.

Standard 4

K.CC.B.4. Understand the relationship between numbers and quantities; connect counting to cardinality.

Standard 5

K.MD.A.1. Describe and compare measurable attributes. Describe measurable attributes of objects, such as length or weight. Describe several measurable attributes of a single object.

Standard 6

K-ESS2-1. Use and share observations of local weather conditions to describe patterns over time. [Clarification Statement: Examples of qualitative observations could include descriptions of the weather (such as sunny, cloudy, rainy, and warm); examples of quantitative observations could include numbers of sunny, windy, and rainy days in a month. Examples of patterns could include that it is usually cooler in the morning than in the afternoon and the number of sunny days versus cloudy days in different months.]

Standard 7

K-ESS3-2. Ask questions to obtain information about the purpose of weather forecasting to prepare for, and respond to, severe weather.

---

can't, if you only use one or two standards for a four- to six-week project. You haven't used your time effectively. We are fortunate enough in the Pre-K to third grade environment to easily connect our literacy standards to authentic projects in creative ways and in short bursts throughout our day. As our learners engage in a challenge, they require many opportunities to demonstrate their understanding of the standards.

We know that you have many standards for which we are responsible for teaching. We also know that these standards are often best taught in a spiraling method, so as to repeat many of them to ensure learner mastery.

Thus, we also advocate for the integration of standards from a variety of content areas. This supports authentic work, as we know that real-world challenges exist outside of the classroom in an integrated manner. As you continue to read through this book, you will find many examples of this.

When we choose multiple standards on which to support our project, we create a deeper project altogether. One or two standards limits the complexity of the work in which our learners may engage. We want our kids to make sense of seemingly disconnected ideas. We want to move from an environment in which we teach separate lessons to one that reframes our approach, focused on the authentic challenge. This helps our learners to string together ideas that may have previously seemed isolated and unrelated.

Now, let's review an example of a relevant and authentic challenge linked to our learners' everyday lives with the standards listed in Figure 2.3. We took a traditional unit on weather and asked how we could connect to our learners' everyday needs and wants. We looked for the standards that connected to these needs and wants. We revisit this example in more depth in Chapters 3 and 4, as we want you to see how the project grows as we move on to other strategies in the book.

We surveyed many of our children and found out they did not have emergency plans or kits in their homes. They only practiced for disasters at school. This provided the relevancy to our challenge. We then used our literacy and science standards to develop an authentic challenge around the weather with a final product of a personalized emergency plan for our learners' homes in the case of a fire, tornado, earthquake, and/or power outages. We also had some of our kids modify the final product by specifically choosing to create emergency plans for their family pets. Their emergency kit included technical instructions via images and emergent text with an emergency evacuation and family exit procedures. We added our technology connection when we asked our learners to create a video to persuade their families/caregivers to design the emergency kit and plan for their own homes. During the challenge implementation, experts such as police officers, firefighters, and members of the state guard/reserves provided feedback to our learners on how to improve their kits.

Questions to Ask When Mapping your Standards to a Project Challenge

As you read through Chapter 1, in what ways did you connect the section on community partnerships to what you already do in your classroom? What activities and projects have you already implemented that you may be able to extend further? While we shared some ideas to jumpstart your thinking (see Table 1.4), now you will want to connect those ideas to your curriculum and standards. At this point, it is a good idea to ask yourself, "how can I maximize both my community assets and authentic challenges my community faces, to bring relevance to my standards and content?" This five step question process will allow you to be successful in designing authentic challenges that are age appropriate, as you implement Strategy One, map standards to the project challenge.

Question 1: To What Challenges in My Community Will My Learners Make Connections and Provide Possible Solutions?

Contrived scenarios are typical in classrooms. A let's pretend approach takes hold and kids jump right into assigned roles. However, this does not leave a lasting impression on our learners nor does it create an experience that requires them to maintain higher levels of critical thinking. Often, scenario-based simulations stop at the applying level of Bloom's. Thus, true authentic learning experiences, for which there is no one right solution, propel our learners to higher cognitive functions.

True authentic projects move our learners beyond just writing about what they research. For example, when given the assignment about what to do about endangered species, a teacher may assign kids to research. They may create a model in art class of an endangered species and write an opinion paragraph about how they would save their endangered species. This example, however, does not push our learners to their highest cognitive potential. We have merely asked for existing research and an analysis of that research. There is no real relevance for completing the activity. Therefore, to make this activity an authentic challenge, we need an authentic community connection. Instead, we ask our learners to create a campaign to adopt a local endangered species and devise a plan to help protect it. When we enlist community feedback and support for our learners' proposed solutions, we give meaning to the challenge. This shifts the focus from an opinion about an animal to moving people to action and makes all the difference in your curriculum.

The alignment of our curriculum to challenges within our community also creates a relevant need for our learners to master the content and skills for which we are responsible to teach. Rather than presenting a disparate set of ideas that our learners struggle to grasp, we now have a concrete approach that is grounded in the real world. This also encourages our kids to view the lens of their community through social action at a developmentally appropriate level. It connects social studies concepts and standards, which are frequently left out or only covered sparingly in the early grade years. Thus, our children are exposed to a richer, more connected curriculum from which they derive personal meaning.

Question 2: What Subject Matter Experts are Available for Consultation in the Design Process and During the Implementation of the Project?

As we previously noted, it is impossible for any of us to be an expert in all of the topics we are required to ensure we incorporate in our classrooms. It may take a little research on your part to identify possible outside experts, either locally or virtually. However, this extra effort pays high dividends. In the Rube Goldberg machine example, we were not engineers. While we certainly understood the standards and the basic physics behind the construction of the machines, we still were not engineers. The engineering students from the local university, however, were able to provide their expertise in the design process. This feedback for our learners was invaluable. It helped them to modify and refine their prototypes until they had perfected their designs to achieve the goals of the challenge. These experts added value to the implementation of the challenge.

It is important to note that not all experts may be a good fit for your classroom. This is where you, the classroom expert, come into play. It may be necessary to provide guidance to a subject matter expert on how to interact with 3 to 9-year-old children. While some may come by it naturally, more often than not we need to provide them with a few basic pointers. In fact, in our experience, we have found this to be true in every expert interaction we have utilized. We want our experts to move beyond the "career day" mentality and that they are only there to give us their job description. We train our experts by prepping them on the authentic projects, the expectation of learner work, and what questions to ask our kids to elicit academic language from their responses. Interaction between our learners and experts provides a wonderful assessment point for us, as the teacher, and is rewarding as we watch our learners use their content knowledge and exhibit mastery of the standards, at a higher level, while engaging with the expert.

Question 3: How Can Products be Learner-Generated and Aligned to My Content and Standards?

As we design our authentic project-based learning experience, it is necessary to have an idea in mind for a final product that is suitable for the audience. This is our summative assessment. As we noted previously, a product is the tangible piece that our learners use to answer or address the challenge. However, it isn't necessary to always require the same final product from each of our learners. Let the kids decide who the final product is for, what the final product looks like, and the shape the final product takes. We just provide them the criteria for the product. The inquiry process will take over from this point.

If we have created an authentic project that is truly open-ended, there will be lots of room for interpretation on how to answer the challenge. It is okay, however, to create set requirements or criteria for these final products. This ensures we can adequately assess the standards included within the challenge. Just as in our Rube Goldberg example, we know our learners need to produce a machine to move the bug-filled marble from one space to another. This provides structure for the challenge, but, at the same time, it does not give a detailed plan for how they will achieve their goal. They must articulate their knowledge of the content in their oral presentations. The ball is pushed using force, gravity pulls the ball downward, and the ball pushes the dominoes over. How our learners build the machine is up to them and the design will likely change as they modify it through a process of feedback from peers, experts, and us.

Classroom doors can be formative presentation spaces with authentic learner work, as well as bathrooms and hallways. Now, the use of pre-made store bought decor is replaced by your learners' divergent thoughts. However, we want to ensure we move beyond merely showcasing the work within our own environment. While this is a fabulous place to begin your journey, challenge yourself and your kids to find excitement and joy in showcasing their final products in other authentic spaces. Connect with local business, your historical society, the local library, or public spaces to become venues. And, don't forget to engage your kids in a conversation about the best potential showcase spots for their work. Trust us, they will have a lot to say!

Question 4: How Can I Incorporate Experts as Part of an Authentic Audience?

All too frequently we turn to parents as the only audience for the work that our learners complete. Authentic learning experiences move us beyond parents and combine the use of familial support with authentic experts. This provides a validation to the final products and to the ways in which the intended audience will use them. Remember, authentic projects end with final products that are designed for use somewhere other than the classroom. Therefore, we see an authentic audience from the perspective of what they have to offer our learners in the possibility of making a solution to the challenge become a reality. We want our audience to have the power to potentially effect the change that has been requested by our children. A solution to the challenge is not as meaningful unless our learners have the opportunity to demonstrate their understanding and mastery of the content knowledge to a stakeholder audience while they simultaneously celebrate their success.

For example, suppose your school's neighborhood has a problem with feral cats. You have several children who don't like going outside for recess in anticipation of seeing a cat or two. Your learners ask you, "What can we do about the cats?" This authentic challenge is the perfect opportunity for your learners to design a solution to the problem and present their findings to the school administration, the local animal shelter, and animal control. While your parents are a great audience, make sure the experts are also a part of the final audience. Your learners create their products for the animal control and animal shelters to help them with a challenge they face. The presence of the authentic audience automatically makes the kids' products real.

This does not mean that the audience must always be present for a formal presentation of learning. It is possible to have our learners send off their final products for review. These may be in electronic form or an actual product that is delivered to a location. In either case, the audience must still be authentic in order for the challenge to be meaningful and effective. A written letter to a local legislator may be more doable, in some cases, than having the legislator actually attend a formal presentation. In either instance, the audience is equally authentic.

Question 5: Does My Community Have any Possible Venues for a Public Presentation?

Not all work that our learners complete is appropriate for a public presentation of learning. However, on the occasions in which it is, you will want to maximize the exposure your learners have outside of the classroom walls. Not only does this provide a more authentic context to the project, but it increases the pride our learners take in the work they complete. One such example includes our public library that might serve as a place for readings of poetry or original stories. Similarly, simply taking our learners on-site to the location in question makes the presentation more authentic for our audience. For instance, a trip to the local historical society for a presentation related to the preservation of our community's past comes alive for our audience, rather than simply inviting them into our classroom space.

We realize the opportunity and/or funds to travel off-site aren't always possible. Planning six to eight months in advance, in order to secure funds, is a daunting idea. However, we can think about virtual opportunities to make this become a reality. A Skype session with experts or a videotaped presentation to send to our audience is an effective alternative. Also, if we secure a location that is willing to showcase products within our community we have created an additional connective layer between our school and our authentic audience. We understand that you have a busy life both inside and outside of school. If you aren't personally able to travel to an off-site location with your kids, perhaps the site would be willing to take the work to showcase by either picking it up or by having you drop it off.

As we noted in the previous step, it isn't always a requirement to have a public presentation of learning. However, we strongly encourage this when possible. Public presentations help our learners to develop and refine their communication skills. It helps them become more comfortable in front of adult audiences and creates a sense of empowerment for a job well done. The addition of an authentic audience helps to accomplish all of these, but moving the venue to outside of the classroom makes the experience that much more memorable for our learners and their audience. This ensures a lasting connection between our learners and their understanding of the content and mastery of the standards in the unit of study.

Our first strategy is the most important. If we fail to start with our standards in mind and map them to our authentic learning experience, we may find the learning gets lost. This is a common complaint of project-based learning and we completely understand why it exists. However, if we start with our standards, the learning is at the forefront of all the work our learners undertake. Rather than merely covering information that may or may not be remembered, now our learners engage in the discovery of new ideas and question old ones. This is where their natural curiosity is piqued and it is up to us to ensure it is maintained throughout the project. What are your next steps? Reflect here, before you move onto the next chapter, on how to create an authentic project challenge for your classroom that meets your standards.

Where are You? What are You Thinking? How do You Feel?		
Take Action	**Seek Community**	**Think Aloud**
Choose two or three standards and develop a challenge idea. Connect to the community resources you identified in Chapter 1 and determine challenges they regularly encounter for which your learners could help find solutions.	Share your idea with a teaching partner and solicit feedback. Be sure to discuss the reasons for the idea and its connection to building more authentic learning experiences in your classroom.	After reading this chapter, what adjustments are you making in your thought processes about the impact of standards demonstrated in a final product? What is one detail that you would like to begin experimenting with right away?

3

Strategy Two: Build Classroom Community

How do I build my classroom community to support the natural curiosity of my learners?

Children are guided by their sense of wonder and curiosity. They naturally ask questions, learn through inquiry, and aspire to make sense of their world around them. Authentic learning experiences permeate the day and the classroom, involving many different curricular areas and skills. These foster a young child's love for learning and exploring. However, when you design authentic projects for your classroom, it does not mean your kids receive the challenge and then have free rein to do what they want. Rather, we mentor our learners through the process to ensure certain skills are mastered along the way. A good mentor creates a community ecosystem that allows for independent work, teamwork, and large and small group instruction. These components vary based upon grade level, but two core items run through every classroom community: routines and schedules. Strategy Two embraces the establishment of routines and schedules to build a classroom community. The goal is to holistically marry our learners' academic, social, and emotional needs as they seek out answers to the wonders of the world around them. This classroom community supports the creativity and innovation promoted in an authentic project approach. This strategy establishes a community of trust and risk-taking which opens the door to help our learners find answers.

How do I build my classroom community to support the natural curiosity of my learners? Let's take a look at the following preschool example to explore how an established classroom community nurtures learner curiosity:

Johnny walks into the classroom enamored with the squirrels that "play race and chase" in the trees outside his classroom window. His excitement causes Arianna to wonder where the squirrels live in their big city. "Where do the squirrels sleep at night?" "What other animals live in the city that are not pets?" Excitement quickly builds as the Pre-K kiddos move toward circle time. Mrs. Smith, their teacher, uses hand gestures and songs to signal the transition. She documents this excitement in a bubble map or discussion web to visualize their thinking and see where they may take their ideas. She encourages her children to draw their ideas and then turn and talk. A shared writing activity captures their questions from their turn and talk. The questions are varied. "What do their beds look like?" "How do they stay warm in the winter?" The class decides to learn about urban wild animals and their homes. The authentic challenge begins to take shape during the morning routine. The Pre-K learners decide they want to create an urban animal home. Mrs. Smith uses the interactive and shared reading time within the daily schedule to link an animal book to their urban animal home designs.[1] This provides the opportunity to observe animal behavior patterns and habitats during the day. The children come up with lots of ideas to explore the animals' homes, what they eat, how they play, and what is scary to the animals in their city. Even before nap/rest time, Mrs. Smith discusses what urban animal beds might feel like.

Each part of the day held a small opportune time to capture the thinking of the kids and use their thoughts as teaching tools throughout the project. The classroom community grew into a learning space where their walls became canvases that corresponded to the learners' developing thoughts, ideas, and possible solutions. The project process is where the learners discovered and uncovered different ways to approach and solve their challenge. The routines and schedules were in place so the children knew they had the autonomy to ask questions, incubate new ideas, and act upon the innovative designs in their imagination.

Just as in the squirrel example, during this time of discovery, our learners explore the purpose of the project, set goals, and begin to organize what details they want to gather to help inform their thinking. We want their learning to be visible and this is the perfect way to begin to build our classroom community. This part of the project process includes the authentic challenge and the questions surrounding it. It also involves the creation of learner teams, team-building exercises, the establishment of a classroom layout to support the project, and the design of centers relevant to the project. All of these important elements build a culture that fosters collaboration and cooperation while deepening the inquiry that must happen during this time of discovery.

This is also a time for your own discovery and finding your own answers. As you shift to an authentic approach in the classroom, the inspiration to ask many questions regarding how your classroom may look and feel will happen. We, too, had questions when we wanted to create a classroom environment in which our learners, like Johnny, felt confident enough to ask questions about the things they wondered about. This took time. When we moved from a more traditional teaching approach to an authentic, learner-centered environment, we needed to find answers to our numerous questions. As we found the answers we realized our schedules and daily routines helped our learners find their own answers.

Let's break down this shift into smaller chunks. As you read this chapter and the rest of this book, as part of your discovery experience you will uncover the answers to your questions. We hope you will continually reflect on these questions as you read. Similarly, as your learners enter into their own authentic challenges, they will also have a myriad of questions that you will want to capture and record. Your role is to support them in finding their answers, as they move closer to determining a solution to the given challenge. You help them organize their thinking along the way. Your classroom and your daily routines become the support your learners need as they move through the authentic challenge. Table 3.1 lists possible questions that might arise when you shift to an authentic approach. Have you asked yourself any of these questions? Have you asked yourself any of these questions?

TABLE 3.1 Possible Questions When You Shift to an Authentic Approach

Learner-Centered Questions: Teacher's Perspective	Learner-Centered Questions: Child's Perspective
What does an authentic classroom look like on a daily basis?	What do I get to play with and create during the day?
Where do authentic projects fit into my schedule with everything else I am required to do?	Do I get to work on my project all day long or do I have to write?
Can preschoolers really do authentic projects?	Can we really make our own stuff?
In what ways do I establish culture in a room of 20–30 preschoolers and kindergarteners?	Will I get to play with all of my friends?
How do my kids work on authentic projects if they cannot read or write?	How will my pictures tell you my story?
How do we establish a community of problem-solvers while maintaining classroom control?	Will I get to choose my favorite ideas?
How do I stay connected with parents about the project and where we are?	What will I take home to show my parents what I am doing?
What are my resources?	What can I use?

To answer the questions requires a partnership between you as a facilitator and your students as learners. Not every authentic challenge can be exactly replicated. Thus, not every question will be answered in the same way for each project you implement.

Take Note: Together, we are in the process of designing an authentic challenge. We scaffold your learning through this chapter's authentic challenge. We model the process throughout this book. Our scaffolding is intentional and an integral part of what we do as teachers; the teaching skills and attitudes do not change during a project.

Just as we use the setup of this book to scaffold for you, you will want to do the same for your own learners. Guide your learners so they get into an inquiry frame of mind on their authentic challenge. This will set them off on the right foot, as you help them to organize their thinking about their solution. At moments of ambiguity, you are there to help clarify where you should push their thinking, but you know when to stop them to add in the scaffolds they need. This provides an environment in which your learners not only gain content knowledge, but also acquire the skills needed to become collaborators and cooperators. It is a gradual release of responsibility for your learners and the rate of release is dependent on the culture of your classroom community and you. Give yourself permission to move as slowly or as quickly as you and your learners need.

We now know that the implementation of an authentic project doesn't mean you let your learners loose and meet them at the finish line. Through the utilization of your schedules and routines, you coach them through their reflection on their progress. This also improves their time management skills and builds their cooperative aptitude. How you structure your routines and daily schedule has a big impact on the support that you provide during the process of the project. The connection between your authentic project and your schedule compliments the development of your classroom community.

Schedules that Support the Project Process

As educators we understand the need for routines and schedules. For authentic challenges, we also understand the need to facilitate content through the project and not teach or frontload all of the content to do the project. Therefore, the schedules and routines play the lead role when making sure projects do not feel like an add-on to your curriculum. We prepare each year knowing that we will need to interactively model and practice our routines many times to ensure our learners are independent, creative, and aware of the expectations throughout the day. This holds true whether you're engaged in an authentic project-based learning experience or in a traditional lesson plan or unit plan.

There are several ways to view your daily schedule in an authentic project. Think about your current schedule and the ways in which it already supports authentic learning.

1   Determine the parts of your day that allow you to create interdisciplinary connections.
2   Identify areas where you already infuse a great deal of inquiry into your lessons.
3   Reflect on your available classroom and school library and how the fiction and nonfiction selections connect to your authentic challenges.
5   Decide how your math concepts work in the real world.

Before you review the sample schedules in Tables 3.2 and 3.3, we want to emphasize that literacy is infused throughout the day and not just completed in one chunk. We take a detailed exploration of early

TABLE 3.2 Sample Pre-K Schedule Aligned to an Authentic Project

Pre-K Schedule	Authentic Community Connections	Johnny's Squirrel Example Project
Schedule breaks and variations include naptime, recess, snack, half-day programs, and other miscellaneous items. Lapses in time, below, account for these breaks.		
8:25–8:40 Morning Meeting/Circle Time	Learners may share a connection to the project. Teacher may connect a short group activity to the project.	Learners share the number of squirrels they saw in the morning.
8:40–8:55 Calendar Math	Establish recording groups and the expectations for learners working together.	Learners record the number of squirrels they see daily.
8:55–9:55 Shared/ Interactive Reading/Book Study	Participate in early literacy activities to build critical thinking skills, shared experiences, and emergent reading skills.	Read books about animals that live in urban areas. Picture walks, art creation, and responding to the text may take place.
10:25–11:00 Morning Centers	Develop routines and structures around dramatic play, blocks, art, and library time to develop their social and emotional community.	Learners connect dramatic play elements to the project. Learners are engaged through dress up clothes, books, and other relevant items.
11:00–12:00 Social Studies or Science through Authentic Projects	Invited experts from the community to lead mini-lessons on science and social studies concepts. Learners engage in science labs related to the project.	Learners work together to create various squirrel home designs using different art materials. A local exterminator talks to the children about how they keep the building safe from squirrels.
2:00–2:45 Afternoon Centers	Management, organization, and routines give learners the opportunity to explore and manage their emotions within their environment.	Centers foster the exploration of habitats and cities through the use of Legos, natural art materials, play corners, and library time.
2:45–3:00 Closing Meeting	Learners may share a connection to the project. Teacher may connect a short group activity to the project.	Share new ideas about their proposed project solutions garnered from the day's activities. Reflect on team participation.

* The schedules uses segments from the Responsive Classroom.

TABLE 3.3 Sample Second Grade Schedule Aligned to an Authentic Project

Second Grade Schedule*	Authentic Community Connections	Classroom Redesign Example Project
8:25–8:40 Morning Meeting/Circle Time	Learners may share a connection to the project. Teacher may connect a short group activity to the project.	Learners share information about the setup of their bedrooms to spark a discussion on how the layout of a room affects the way in which we interact in that room.
8:40–8:55 Math Computation and Review	Practice concepts previously learned to reinforce skills. Write word problems that utilize project vocabulary and concepts.	Practice measurement through sample floor plans, floor plans from home, and the new classroom floor plan.
8:55–9:55 Reader's Workshop	Participate in various literacy activities to build critical thinking skills, shared experiences, and emergent reading skills. Conduct a word study to focus on high frequency, compound, multisyllabic, amazing, rare, or wow words.	Read books about architecture. Fiction texts such as *Young Frank, Architect* and *Iggy Peck Architect* build the skills to "identify how characters in a story respond to major events and challenges." (RL.2.3)
10:25–11:00 Writer's Workshop	Participate in writing activities such as developing a personal narrative, expository, opinion/argument, or informational writing piece.	Develop a writing piece meant to persuade, inform, or reflect on redesigning their classroom.
11:00–12:00 Social Studies or Science through Authentic Projects using … Reading Skills: Read to self, write to self, read to partner. Writing skills: writing, editing and publishing	Invited experts from the community to lead mini-lessons on science or social studies concepts. Learners engage in science labs related to the project and connect their learning back to the challenge through reading, writing, reflecting and partner talk.	Use ideas from *Archi-Doodle* to inspire social studies and science lessons that include sustainability issues, reading plans, designing spaces, and choosing sites and materials. Invite a local architect and an interior designer to engage in a conversation with the kids about designing spaces. Read *Built to Last* to discover some of the world's greatest architecture.
1:00–2:00 Math Instruction, Math Workshop, and Math Learning Stations	Connect small portions of math concepts to the project through "do nows", exit tickets, and quizzes. Write word problems that utilize project vocabulary and concepts.	Lesson on measurement that has kids predict the length of various things in the classroom and then measure them to get an accurate length.

| 2:45–3:00
Closing Meeting | Learners may share a connection to the project. Teacher may connect a short group activity to the project. | Share new ideas about their proposed project solutions garnered from the day's activities.
Reflect on team participation. |

*The schedule uses segments from the Responsive Classroom.

literacy through authentic projects in Chapter 4, but first, let's look at examples of schedules that support authentic project implementation.

Make small shifts to your schedule to begin to build a culture of community in your classroom and still maintain the classroom routines that are important to our young learners. Embed opportunities to promote inquiry throughout your daily routine to encourage your learners' natural curiosity to ask deep questions, rather than subdue it. In fact, if you view your entire teaching day as one full opportunity to extend a learning experience, rather than as a segmented one, it increases the depth in which your learners delve into an authentic learning experience. These become the learning experiences they remember for years to come. It also sets the stage for their success in the later elementary grades and beyond.

As you establish your classroom community, we recommend you take notes on what happens and reflect on your notes—when possible. For example, in Chapter 6, we talk about intrinsic motivation, which impacts how your kids work within a group. If you keep anecdotal notes on behaviors, you can reflect on your classroom community and ways to continually improve the performance of your learners. This allows you to adjust classroom routines in real time. It also sets you up for success the next time you desire to begin a project. In fact, a good first challenge might be to have your learners determine what it means to be a classroom community and how they are a part of it. It could also be a whole school challenge, with each grade level taking a portion of the focus. This is similar to the typical theme of "Welcome Back to School" or "All About Me" that begins a new school year. This authentic challenge is an excellent way to invite your kids into the process of establishing classroom routines. It provides your learners with a voice so they take ownership in the creation of that classroom community. This project also aligns with social studies content related to citizenship, identifying classroom jobs, and identifying similarities and differences among people. As we begin to build self-directed readers and writers, it also supports your learners as they approach each new authentic challenge with a deeper set of questions and a greater sense of autonomy.

Scaffolding to Support Your Daily Routines

Break down your project into smaller pieces to help you manage your daily routines and schedule. When you decide to implement an authentic project, you shouldn't feel as though it is something totally new. While you may feel overwhelmed at the prospect, feel confident in the skills you have already acquired as a teacher. They will help you begin your exciting journey. You already plan your instruction using the strategies listed in this book. The result of linking these strategies together is an authentic project that builds the capacity of your learners as problem-solvers who are confident in their ability to find a solution.

Authentic work still relies on the use of routines and scaffolding. It utilizes your ability to mentor your kids through the learning experience. The classroom management tools you currently use directly fit into the overall and daily life of the challenge. In fact, they help to ensure the project runs smoothly. You design a learning experience to move through the content in an authentic way. The content now goes from random activities to purposeful projects with your lesson planning focused on purposeful design. As you embark on the experience, the instructional methods and strategies you already use also support your learners in finding a solution to the challenge (Table 3.4).

These routines are an excellent way to help build academic language (see Figure 1.1) and implement the types of thinking that align with where your learners are within a project. As you scaffold your teaching activities throughout your daily routine, the complexity gains momentum and your lessons build upon each other, leading to deeper understanding over time. We always like to reiterate and remember that in the beginning of a project-based learning experience, your learners will not know what to do. The project may feel as if it is not going anywhere so we have to allow our children to learn through the questions they generate and create the space for them to generate the questions. For now, if you allow uncertainty, you help your learners use their concrete and representational tools (i.e. manipulatives and drawing) to connect what they think to what they can touch.

Empower your learners to integrate the concepts that are contextualized in their work through what they draw, write, build, or construct. These representations make up the data needed for learners to demonstrate what they know and what they can do with the challenge they have been given. Instructional methods and activities are repeated to show growth in knowledge and skills as the project progresses. In fact, as you incorporate these into your daily routine, you provide your learners with the opportunity to master the skills, standards, and content in your grade level requirements.

TABLE 3.4 Classroom Routines Support Success in Finding a Solution

Routines	Support for Authentic Project
Morning Routine: Around the Circle, Dialogue Sharing, Current Events	Children are encouraged to explore, draw, and record questions to support inquiry related to the challenge.
Independent Work Time	Abundant play, reading, and prototyping opportunities are available for learners to interact with literacy and numeracy.
Read-Alouds, Interactive Reading, Shared Reading	Children are given many authentic and meaningful opportunities to interact with literacy.
Transitions	Create a connection between vocabulary words, related songs, and hand signals to relate to the authentic challenge. For example, when studying butterflies, put your hands together into a butterfly shape to create a signal for that unit.
Learning Centers	Opportunities for differentiated and personalized learning time, as well as direct one-on-one or small group teaching and reading intervention are present.

Schedules and Routines as Scaffolds in Learning

Routines play an important part in your classroom environment. They help you manage groups, identify scheduling opportunities, and scaffold the learning in a project. Create the scaffolds for your authentic challenge and use the verbs from Bloom's Taxonomy to ask appropriately leveled questions (Table 3.5). Throughout the life of the project and on a daily basis, you determine the levels in which your learners are engaged. Your routines provide the time frames for when you implement the appropriate and needed resources for your kids. These include concept maps, guides, and time to model tasks through the coaching of either social or cognitive skills. Remember, it is okay to be the teacher and the guide in this process. You are still very important and your learners need you. Eventually, you won't need to scaffold as much toward the end of the project as you did during the start of it.

Review the following examples and explore how they used authentic project-based learning to build a classroom community and ensure all learners exhibit growth through the project. Feel free to adapt a project concept to meet your own grade level standards and requirements. It is easy to deepen the complexity of a project for older learners or to provide additional supports for younger kids.

TABLE 3.5 Scaffolding Examples through Bloom's Taxonomy*

Bloom's Taxonomy	Project Question Scaffolds	Schedule	Routine
Creating	How can we develop a machine from recycled materials that moves objects?	Science Reader's Workshop Writer's Workshop	Combine all the parts together to develop a product and presentation.
Evaluating	Does my Rube Goldberg machine show my understanding of force, motion, and the engineering design process to my intended audience members?	Science Reader's Workshop Writer's Workshop Technology Class Math	Judge the effectiveness of their designs by testing and collecting data on the number of successes and number of times it failed.
Analyzing	How will my design ideas change if I increase the number of pushes and pulls?	Science Reader's Workshop Writer's Workshop Math	Conduct a lab exploring force and motion.
Applying	Based on my inferences and research, am I applying enough force to create motion with my marble?	Reader's Workshop Math Science	Read nonfiction books about ramps, push, and pull. Make ramps using geometric shapes in math. Create small Rube Goldberg samples and count the number of pushes and pulls in science.
Understanding	Have I selected the right information to begin designing my first machine prototype?	Reader's Workshop: This does not need to be the entire reader's workshop. It can be 15 minutes of a reader's workshop over a three- to five-day period. Science : Learners do their research during this time.	Research anchor charts and make it a part of the routine to review/practice the anchor chart before they collect data.
Remembering	What important information do I need to know to begin working on my challenge?	Morning meeting to make connections to authentic challenge.	Connect a group activity to the project. This can be a five-minute activity such as Word of the Day or Scan for Vocabulary Tools.

* We have used the Rube Goldberg example from Table 2.2.

Pre-K: How Do We Curate our School Like a Museum?

We wanted to give our Pre-K children the opportunity to turn our school into a museum. Our project goals were to teach handwriting through art, improve fine motor skills through design, and embed math through literacy. Over a four-week period, we followed this process of scaffolding and embedded the project into our daily routine. Keep in mind, we actually posed the question and used the word curate. We had to unpack this word by showing our learners a video and books about the curator of a museum and how they hang the picture collections. Later, they learned all about exhibits. We specifically mention this fact, because we don't want you to limit yourself by thinking that a word might be too big for your kids. It isn't. We simply have to provide the appropriate scaffolds to help them unpack the meaning of curate in a visual and simple way.

To officially invite our learners into the challenge we did several things. We strategically placed a bunch of art books around the room to encourage self-exploration. Similarly, we provided pictures of museums and art tools. To bring the outside community into the classroom, we invited a few artists as guest speakers. We let our learners explore the materials, talk to the artists, and play with the tools. We then let them go into centers and explore all things related to museums and art. We read them stories like *Jack in Search of Art* by Arlene Boehm about how Jack the Bear wanders through a museum in search of "Art." His search becomes a virtual tour as he encounters wonderful paintings and sculptures, which are actually digitized photographs of masterpieces from Wyeth, Rosetti, Hopper, Calder, and more—each cleverly set into the illustrations. We then asked our Pre-K children how they could turn our school into a museum. Many of the children said, "Us? You want us to do it? But, how?"

Over the next four weeks, learners connected the basic elements of shape (the line, dot, circle, angle, and the curve) to various art pieces, letters, and their physical surroundings. As they uncovered the basic elements of shape in their everyday world, they began to see how their world takes shape through these five basic elements. The children then chose a piece of art to create and identified the basic elements of shape they wanted to include. They drew their first drafts in black crayon on white paper. They presented these drafts to their peers, pointing out the basic elements of shape. During this time we created centers that connected to the basic elements of shape. The art center had items for the children to use in the shapes of the elements. The block center focused on building with the basic elements of shape. The dramatic play center was changed throughout the four weeks to hold various art tools, art mediums, and dress up. The interactive reading, shared reading, and read-alouds connected to all things art. Our kids read about Frida Kahlo, Pablo Picasso, and street art we found in our city. Our math centers focused on the basic elements of shape and connected one-to-one correspondence and counting to famous pieces of art and in our everyday wonderful stories. We asked a multitude of questions: How many stars can we count in Van Gogh's *Starry Night*? How many pieces can we count in Gaudi's *Salamander*? Each day, the children added a little more to their own drafts. The second draft was then presented to local artists who gave our children feedback and showed them basic artist tricks to enhance their own works. Our learners, with a week and a half to go, began their final canvases, using their intended arts tools. We had them create watercolors, mosaics, and a mix of mediums. We provided the learning opportunities, but our children created the designs. The only piece that was teacher-generated were the cardboard frames that each child decorated, as we felt it was still too early to give them box cutters. In the end, we hung all their artwork around the school just like you would see in an exhibit. Parents were able to view the artwork during our school's parent-teacher conferences over a period of three weeks. On the back of each canvas we taped each child's first and second draft so parents could see the growth in their child's work. Each child signed their piece of art—with their own masterpiece, their name. These masterpieces were then sent to a local gallery as a special showcase for the month. The pièce de résistance was their feelings of pride when they saw their work displayed in their community.

Kindergarten: How Do We Create a Survival Kit Campaign for our Parents and Caregivers?

Most kindergarten children study weather, but we wanted our kids to do more than just study weather. We asked ourselves how we could make weather relevant to our learners. We wanted to turn science concepts, math standards, and English Language Arts (ELA) into an authentic trifecta of fun. Since our community experiences natural disasters that range from flooding, severe thunderstorms, severe hailstorms, and ice storms to tornados, we wanted to create a project that had long-lasting effects on our learners and their families. Our hope was to move beyond the "what clothes we wear during which season" and "cotton ball clouds" lessons to create a useful product for families.

Through a basic family questionnaire, we learned that most families did not have an emergency survival kit or an emergency evacuation plan where they live. This was our first opportunity to connect our learners' life outside of school to the project. Whether living in a home or an apartment, everyone needs to be prepared in all weather-related emergencies. This was the spark for our challenge idea. To develop the idea and ground it in the curriculum, we used the Next Generation Science Standards, Common Core State Standards for math, reading, and writing (see Figure 2.3). In an effort to maximize our time, we merged all of these standards into one project. We saw the need to draw on our learners' use of nonfiction text to make inferences. All of the interdisciplinary components led to a connected daily schedule where the challenge was anchored in our ELA time, but also interjected in our math, reading, writing, and transitions.

We brought in the fire department and a high school counselor to introduce the authentic challenge. They shared their stories about how they helped others during an emergency, both physically and emotionally. They challenged our children to create their own kits and plans at their house. They also announced they would be back to check on their progress, in a few weeks, to provide feedback on their prototypes.

For the final product, we chose to have our learners create a persuasive online video for family members or caregivers to view, to convince them of the reasons why they needed an emergency evacuation plan and emergency kit in their home. They also had to create an actual emergency kit. During this time, their homework routines also revolved around the challenge. For example, during one week, we required them to bring back a drawing of their home that had evacuation routes and a picture of a possible survival kit they could build. They had to explain why they chose the items in their kits and how they would maintain their them.

The children began to map the weather during morning meeting, study the types of natural disasters in the area, look at rainfall numbers, and chart various other forms of precipitation, such as hail, over a period of time. During our reader's workshop, they learned about the Farmer's Almanac, read nonfiction texts about weather, and gathered information. Our learners read, wrote, and articulated their thoughts in whole group and small group discussions, and individually throughout their day. They used their information to create a 2-D prototype and a list of items that would be included in their kits. We brought in the Texas State Guard to give the kids feedback on their kit ideas. The simple ways we modified our schedules and routines to support the project led to a finished product that brought meaning to the lives of our children while simultaneously bringing the weather content to life for them.

First Grade: How Can We Design Sound Installations for our Playground?

The science standards on light and sound and literacy standards on reading informational text were the foundation for this project challenge and it was one that we knew could easily pique our learners' interests. Before we brought our kids into the challenge and to more fully formulate the challenge in our own minds, we walked around our school. In our morning, recess, and after school walks, we listened for the sounds and sights that our kids made in the halls, on the playground, and in the cafeteria. We came to the conclusion that we heard no musical sounds while the Pre-K and kindergarten kids played outside. Thus, the decision to plan the project around kids creating a sound installation for the playground was made.

To prepare for the information and prototyping stage, we gathered all of our fiction and nonfiction music, sound, vibration, light, and songbooks from our classroom library. Our librarian also helped to gather books and became a resource and an expert for the project. We decided that light was not to be a part of the kids' installations, as it would be too complicated for them. However, we knew we needed to embed the light information within the project to reinforce the sound concepts.

To launch the project, we read a book about our five senses. Then, we took the class outside on a sound and light walk. We asked our kids to record what they saw, heard, smelled, and touched; we skipped taste. After their walk, they did a formal journal reflection that included both a drawing and a written piece to describe what they experienced. Next, we had the school principal come into our class and ask our kids for their help in designing a sound installation for the playground. Our learners instantly asked questions and wondered about what, where, when, and how. We gave our kids notecards and had them capture all their thoughts and questions. Then, we spent the next few days doing research on sounds and vibrations and they began to sketch out their ideas. Based on our kids' ideas and initial designs, we met with our building maintenance man and asked for any leftover materials he could offer for the project. These included small, but dull metal pieces, any type and size of PVC pipe, washers, screws, jar tops, and anything else that could potentially be used to make sound. We also went to the large home improvement supply stores in our city to collect small pieces of chain, scrap PVC pipe, and any other materials we could get for free. With all of our materials, our kids began to design their sound installations with the knowledge they had gained about sounds and vibration. For this challenge, they were required to make three different sounds per installation. With our audience in mind, each sound also had to be capable of being manipulated by a young child.

On the first day of feedback, we brought in the actual users of their final product and had them test their prototypes. It was a perfect learning moment because our first graders were in total awe of how rough the Pre-K kids were while playing with their sound installations. Our first graders kept telling the kids to be gentle and to not play too roughly with their designs. When the ten-minute session was up, our first graders looked visibly upset. This led our kids to have a great discussion about strength, sturdiness, and the longevity of their designs. Collectively, they decided their designs should last three weeks and be able to withstand any weather conditions. Later in that same week, we brought in the music teacher to give a lesson on vibration and let the kids make sounds using instruments. Our weekly homework required our kids to create a straw or any other type of material flute for a class performance that was to take place during our morning meeting.

We spent the next week troubleshooting our sound installation designs, based on our first round of feedback. We had our teams deconstruct and reconstruct their designs. Many of them expressed how they wished they had taken pictures of the kids playing. As we pushed through that minor setback, we continued to read and write about our experiences every step of the way and used their project process journals as formal and informal assessments. They glued the content, team, and writing rubrics in their notebooks. They then assessed themselves as teammates, engineers, and writers to visually see how they moved along the rubric continuum, as they maintained or improved their level of success. During this time, our kids deliberated their point of view and their audience's point of view to ensure the installations were just right for them. As we finished our designs, our kids wrote letters to our building Operations Manager to ask him for help in the installation of their designs. Once he agreed, we met with him to figure out where they could be installed. He brought blueprints of the school so our kids could decide on the various possible locations. The kids walked around the school with such purpose as they looked for the potential locations. Our Operations Manager also showed them how he could help install each team's product. For this, he gave them two options for installation: cable ties or a hammer and nails. They then had two days to make sure their installations were ready for the install date and the Pre-K and kindergarten unveiling. The intensity of the building looked and felt like play as they laughed and sang as they worked. As their final presentation, our learners went around to the different classrooms to demonstrate their installations and explain why their three sounds produced vibrations. All in all, the day vibrated with excitement as our kids made music all around the school. Our first graders felt not only more connected to their installations, but a deeper connection was formed between the two grade levels as they shared a common piece of the school.

Second Grade: How Can We Redesign our Classroom to Better Meet our Needs?

Is there a better way to improve the learning environment for your kids than to ask them specifically how to do it? This challenge was born out of the need for one of our teachers to change classrooms for the following year. In fact, it wasn't just changing classrooms across the hall, but the K–2 building was set to close and we were slated to move into the 3–5 building. We decided, in order to better serve the needs of our future second graders, we should ask our current second graders what was working, what wasn't working, what they wanted, what they needed, and what we could do to better support them. Rather than just stop at that, we asked them to completely redesign their classroom.

To set the project in motion, we took a field trip down the road to the new building. We invited our kids to walk around the building and their future classrooms to generate new ideas and excitement. We asked them to keep in mind how they would use natural light versus light from an electrical source. We asked them to use their five senses and take a sensory walk around the space and think about details, similar to the process of what we do in our writer's workshop. A visit to multiple classrooms allowed them to generate additional ideas and see the school from a broader perspective. The trip to these classrooms helped them to see the school from a variety of viewpoints, which was helpful as a reflection in the later stages of the challenge. In the specific second grade classrooms, they took pictures, measured the rooms, sketched out the current layout, and brainstormed ideas for the redesign. We asked our kids to imagine themselves as they carried their bags through the hallway and entered their soon to be classrooms. When we got back to our school, our kids decided they should also question the first graders about the things they wanted in their classroom, as they would be the actual ones to use the classroom in the following year. For this task, they developed a short questionnaire and then created bar, circle, and pictographs to represent the responses.

Our learners then worked in small teams to design specific sections of the classroom. We first discussed how they would work together. As teachers, we knew that it would be too difficult for them as an entire class, as a big team, to collaborate effectively. However, we let them come to this conclusion through a guided discussion. They decided that all 23 kids working as a big group was just too much. They then split themselves into assigned groups for the reading corner, learning stations, small group learning area, technology area, work on writing area, and storage areas. These were based on their personal areas of interest. We also decided not to limit them to just these conventional areas. We challenged our kids to think about additional areas they believed would enhance their learning experience. We wanted them to see beyond their traditional work zones and imagine themselves playing and learning all around their building. Thus, in addition to their one assigned traditional classroom area, they were asked to pitch a secondary idea. The result was every idea imaginable from an indoor garden and an outdoor classroom to a makerspace and a classroom mini-kitchen.

Next, our groups of kids worked together to create a presentation for the first graders who would be learning in the new classroom for the following year. These first graders gave our learners end user feedback for them to refine their ideas. From this feedback, the changes made were then compiled for a final presentation to a panel that included our building administrator and district superintendent. Some of the ideas our kids proposed included flexible seating, lamps instead of only overhead lighting, and desks that could be flipped and used as presentation boards. While not every change was possible, as we moved into the building the following year, the voice that our learners had in truly designing their classroom community permeated the room.

Third Grade: How Can We Design a Quilt that Tells a Story?

This project, designed by Jerry Ann Brown of Elkin Elementary in Elkin, NC, was developed in an effort to embed multiple content areas in an authentic challenge that was launched through literacy. The project challenge reached the initial content goal, but also generated a special, heartwarming ending when the children were able to use their final product to raise money for a special community member. They handed their hard-earned money to a teacher assistant from their school who was battling cancer. What started as an authentic challenge tuned into an act of kindness that also made them aware of their ability to care for someone and be empathetic. Jerry Ann worked hard to develop an authentic challenge that met the required standards and the content for which she was responsible, but also wanted to ensure that the social and emotional development of her class would bolster her classroom culture. Once we had the opportunity to observe part of it in action, we knew we had to share it with you.

After a great deal of design work to align her content and standards to an authentic idea, Jerry Ann settled on quilting as a guiding theme. Since Elkin is a tight-knit community, she knew quilting was something that many of her kids would personally relate to from either a church connection or a direct family member who was a quilter. In fact, a quilter from the community brought several of her quilts for the class to observe. She also read Johnston's *The Quilt Story* to them. The children asked her questions about quilting, the patterns they observed from the quilts, and what she did with the quilts once they were made. However, before the guest speaker arrived, to set this project in motion and launch the inquiry process, the class was divided into small groups and directed to read a fiction book specifically related to quilting. However, the kids were not told the books were all about quilting. Collectively, Ms. Brown's kids read their given books and determined the setting, main characters, main events, problem, and solution. Following the reading, the class did a gallery walk of the posters with the required information. This was for them to observe the summaries of the other books without the need to read all of the books. Once the whole class came back together, they were asked if they could determine the common thread between all of the books: quilting. This discussion led the kids into discovering the reasons behind quilting. These two main activities led into the project challenge that was given to the class: to design a class quilt to be raffled off with the proceeds given to a charity of their choice.

Throughout much of the year, various standards and content related to the third grade-pacing guide were tied back to the quilting theme. During Black History Month, the class read *Sweet Clara and the Freedom Quilt* by Deborah Hopkinson. To connect deeply to the writing process, the school librarian conducted a lesson that asked the children to create their own story about a quilt. Throughout a unit on geometry, the design of the quilts was related to plane figures. The class even watched the *Reading Rainbow* show, "Patchwork Quilt." This specifically tied into to a discussion on the importance the book's family placed on quilts and the design of Tanya's quilt in the show, and, ultimately, led to a brainstorming session on what the design of the class quilt should look like. From these ideas, the class voted on the top three ideas presented.

To complete the class quilt, Ms. Brown contacted several quilters from the community to volunteer to help sew together the final design for the class quilt. Even though they only had one sewing machine in the school's makerspace, the children were all given the opportunity to try their own hand at sewing. Additionally, to connect to the community beyond the school, the local paper was contacted to do a community interest story on the class quilt. This also helped to advertise the sale of the raffle tickets which was to take place during the following school year's open house.

As the children learned, the act of quilting is a special thing and has deep meaning connected to it. From the designs to the actual quilting process, it is a labor of love and has a story to tell. In fact, when asked, many of the kids reflected that the stories they read and the stories they were told were the best part of the project. To that end, we are sure these children will someday have their own stories to tell their children about this authentic project-based learning experience.

Collaborative and Cooperative Grouping within Your Classroom Community

Our young learners flourish in environments that foster their natural curiosity and build their skills while giving them autonomy, safety, and flexibility. As we implement authentic challenges in our classrooms, we provide the opportunities for our learners to increase their socio-emotional health and build the emotional intelligence constructs they need to become adept problem-solvers later in life.

Even at the ages of 4 and 5, our young learners have the ability to help each other make decisions and solve problems, as a team. Each year, this ability increases. There are several things we can do to facilitate this process to ensure our kids move from the completion of simple group work in a semi-collaborative setting to a cooperative team environment that adds value to our classroom community.

In the beginning of the Pre-K and kindergarten school year, we start with small groups of two in an authentic challenge and increase the group size as we move through the school year. This gives us the chance to build a classroom community where our young learners move from being aware of just themselves to becoming aware of others in their group. As we foster this awareness of self-to-self and self-to-group, in our classrooms, we encourage our learners to become more empathetic to themselves and the members of their team. We plan the structure, procedure, and the execution of team development throughout the project to ensure our kids have the mental models, pictures in their minds, and time to practice group techniques.

As our teams move through the Stages of Finding a Solution, we observe and sometimes record their social and emotional ability. We do this to provide growth-producing feedback, both individually and to teams, so they learn to mitigate their emotions and develop their interpersonal skills. We support our teams as they work to find alternative and new ways of communicating. This is especially important for our English Language Learner (ELL) and dual language populations as they acquire new language skills.

Beyond the beginning of kindergarten, we like our group sizes to stay between two and four as they gain the communication, cooperative, and collaborative skills to effectively work their way through the group dynamics that exist at each Stage of Finding a Solution. However, it depends on our project and what the project challenge has asked our kids to complete. The older our learners are, the more comfortable we are with a larger group size and they become more adept in their interpersonal and collaborative skill sets.

In order to develop the collaborative skills needed to function well in a team, we want to ensure the cooperative activities strategically match the Stage of Finding a Solution. An aligned cooperative learning structure or procedure we implement, that matches a team's needs during a particular stage, supports positive group dynamics. The boost to interpersonal skills, the increase in confidence for individual kids, and the deeper academic learning that result are added benefits when we incorporate authentic learning experiences in our classrooms.

There are several activities we like to use to facilitate good teaming skills in the first stage of a project. The Yarn–Yarn activity is a great visual to help our learners see what teamwork looks like. This structure provides a record of interaction patterns that we use to debrief how a collaborative conversation should unfold. We start off with a prompt, related to the challenge, to get the discussion flowing and the only material we need is a ball of yarn. As we begin the process, each time a team member wants to talk, he/she must wrap the yarn around his/her finger. At the end of the conversation, the visual provides information for reflection on who did the most or the least amount of talking. We also start to unravel the yarn to peel away the layers of the conversation. This process, and many others we have listed in Appendix 1, helps our kids to build team skills without taking time out of our day to do an activity that is unrelated to our authentic challenge.

As our teams move into Stage 2, to gather information and develop prototypes, it becomes ever apparent that they need to work together to share their information. Information gleaned from one individual may strengthen another's ideas. This means, all of our learners are involved in the process of gathering information to produce a prototype. Here, we like to use the Roving Reporter for several reasons. A child who acts as the reporter gains a sense of confidence in their assigned role, as it is an important job. The role is easily shared by teammates, as they switch off during the different days of the project. Also, this provides interaction between our teams and creates a deeper sense of community within our classrooms. This helps our kids to see the project is not a competition between teams, but they are, in fact, working toward the same end goal.

In each stage of an authentic challenge, it is important not only to align collaborative activities to our learners' needs, but also to celebrate the successes and setbacks of teams, as they grow. This type of reflection helps our learners identify how they feel as a member of a group and articulate what makes them feel good. They then are able to transfer those feelings to how they treat their teammates. We use several activities to support our teams and make their growth visual. The Start, Stop, Continue method is a tool that reinforces the needs of each team member and the class as a whole. Each member of the team shares what they want to start doing, what they want to stop doing, and what they want to continue doing. This activity provides reassurance and actionable feedback, and is a quick way to show that all teams have areas of growth and many reasons to celebrate. This particular activity also helps our learners to consider the viewpoints of others. Thus, it is a perfect addition to the Perspective and Point of View Stage.

Once we move into Stage 4, the cooperative spirit necessary to push toward the end of the project is as important as it was to launch the project. Here, we tap into the critical thinking necessary to successfully consider the consequences of one's actions. In order to also foster the creativity we strive to enhance in our young learners, we use the Pass Around Strategy. For this, we have our team members collaborate to write a story. We simply provide a prompt to begin the process. We prefer to use a prompt that is the start of a scenario related to the challenge. From this, our kids build up the story and determine the actions the characters take, as well as the consequences of those actions. Each member of the team takes a turn at crafting a sentence. Here, critical thinking is necessary, as our kids must work together to formulate a story that makes sense. Creativity is also paramount, as blending all of the sentences, from each member of the team, into a story that is engaging for the reader takes ingenuity. This activity helps to build strong writers, as they think about cohesion and coherence, just as they must do with their project challenge.

Now that the project is nearing completion, in Stage 5, we like to bring together our groups for a final discussion. While many options exist for a discussion protocol, our twist on the Socratic Seminar is well placed, here. Appendix 1 details the process of the Socratic Seminar, but there are a few things to keep in mind. Our younger learners are not always ready to conduct a full class discussion. We sometimes have to break them into smaller sub-groups that represent two or three teams. If we have older kids, or our younger kids are used to this process, we can create a whole class discussion. The Socratic Seminar, at this stage, is a good point of reflection for teams to identify any missing components of their solution. As they affinity map the discussion, they see patterns in the conversation that usually represent shortcomings with their ideas. The conversation also provides a space to confirm any ideas that they have and does so from a broader perspective. Since our learners have worked in smaller teams or pairs for much of the project, this activity opens the classroom culture to include the voices of all our children.

Our classroom community is the place where our young children learn to be successful in their environments. Together, they safely practice the self-regulatory and management tools that foster not only their natural curiosity, but also the collective natural curiosity of the team. Intentional collaboration provides the space for our learners to improve their work continuously, over time. It also deepens the result of the authentic challenge as our children collectively grow and learn.

Embed Technology to Support Daily Routines and Build Classroom Community

Our youngest learners, today, bring a whole new meaning to the term "digital native," coined a decade and a half ago by Marc Prensky. Many have already mastered tablet devices, smartphones, and even simple laptop computer maneuvers. Thus, when we create an authentic learning experience embedded with technology supports, we make the experience more relevant for even our youngest children. The use of strategically chosen technology programs, apps, and management systems have the ability to provide a variety of scaffolds. If you are in search of content rich material, skills practice, classroom management help, or communication with others, there are more resources available than one can manage to keep straight. We have listed just a few of our favorites in Table 3.6. Feel free to explore the options that are available to you. If your technology resources are limited, consider applying for a grant to increase the number of devices in your classroom.

It is important to remember that any use of technology with children under the age of 13 is strictly regulated by several government guidelines. This may be easy to overlook when using the technology for educational purposes, since a great deal of our learners have had devices in their hands from a very young age. Many of our learners even have their own tablet devices. In fact, we have seen children as

TABLE 3.6 Tech Tools

Technology Tool	Application of the Tool
Animoto	Digital storytelling and presentation app
BrainPop Jr.	Short, engaging videos and activities on a variety of topics
Class Dojo	Classroom management platform to encourage positive behavior and keep parents up to date on learner progress
Kidblog	Safely upload learner blog posts and allow kids to reply to posts
Remind	Communication with parents about upcoming events
Planbook	Lesson planning that can be shared between teachers and allow your learners to view online
Project Foundry	Management system designed specifically for project-based learning experiences
Seesaw	Audio and video homework and newsletters
Symbaloo	Social bookmarking site for easy learner access that is a visual cue to needed links
ZooBurst	Create 3-D visual pop-up books

young as second grade with mobile phones. However, let's pause to take a look at these guidelines and their effect on our classroom use of technology (Table 3.7).

Whether you have access to a great deal of technology or no technology at all, the shift to an authentic approach in the classroom may inspire you to ask many questions regarding how your classroom could look and feel throughout the day. As you read through the rest of this book to find your answers:

1   What will you do differently?
2   What shifts are you personally experiencing?
3   How will your learners feel an immediate connection to their community (classroom or beyond)?
4   Do you want it to be gradual or to change things up quickly?

You know your learners best. Don't be afraid to invite your learners into the process and ask them how they would design a project for the class. Just like we did with our second graders, question them as to how they might shift the classroom layout to accommodate a new project or in which part of the day they want more autonomy. The examples we have just provided are designed to empower you to embark on your own discovery of ways to continue to embrace the natural curiosity of your learners. Many of us already have tools and resources in our classroom so small tweaks and additions to our daily routines and schedules make a huge impact as we build our classroom community to support our learners in the project process.

TABLE 3.7 Technology Guidelines to Follow

Federal Guideline	Implications for Classroom Use
Children's Internet Protection Act (CIPA)	Restricts access to obscene or harmful content when Internet sites are used for children. Libraries and schools that receive discounts for Internet access or connections through the E-Rate program must comply with this.
Children's Online Privacy Protection Act (COPPA)	Children under the age of 13 may not share their personal information over the Internet without expressed consent from a parent or guardian.
Family Educational Rights and Privacy Act (FERPA)	Protects the privacy of education records.

As you begin your authentic journey to transform your classroom environment, in order to implement Strategy Two and build a classroom community, there may be bumps in the road. Each group of learners and each authentic project will bring new challenges. Establish a supportive classroom environment with a consistent, but not always the same, routine to allow your learners to build ownership of their project process. As they change and learn so does the community and culture. Trust is built during times of change and we model how to accept change and learn with it, rather than simply from it. Most importantly, remember to continually reflect on your own learning. What are your next steps? Reflect here, before you move onto the following chapter, on how to build your classroom community to support the natural curiosity of your learners.

Where are You? What are You Thinking? How do You Feel?		
Take Action	**Seek Community**	**Think Aloud**
Choose two or three areas within your daily schedule where you could begin to provide your learners with more autonomy in the authentic challenge. Experiment and practice with these changes to your routines. Document your learners' reactions to the changes.	Share your changes with a teaching partner and solicit feedback. Be sure to discuss the ways in which the change would support the authentic learning experience you began working on in Chapters 1 and 2.	After reading this chapter and reflecting on previous schedule changes you have made, how are those adjustments different than the authentic adjustments you would like to make? Reflect on how you respond to change and how your learners respond to changes.

Note

1   In alignment with this project, the second grade classes decided
    to create urban animal observation decks, for use by the
    younger students, to be placed around the school campus.

4

Strategy Three: Make Reading and Writing Authentic

How can I use literacy skills to support authentic learning experiences?

We want our kids to love reading! We want them to be fluent enough to comprehend everything they read. Levels of literacy achievement set the stage for success or struggle throughout a child's educational career. The greater the foundations for reading and writing, the more prepared our learners are for the world ahead. A child who loves to read connects to what they like. That child has the skills, time, and space to share their excitement and joy about what they interpret. They are able to communicate and connect their own lives to literary characters or through the facts they uncover with every new page. Thus, the symbolic behaviors (reading, writing, drawing, singing, dancing, acting, and storytelling) for a successful reader and writer require our learners to do several things. They must demonstrate their abilities to interpret, evaluate, and communicate meaning of content and its impact on the world around them. We want our children to be aware that play and talk can easily be transformed into something they read or they write. Symbolic representations are placed on a literacy-based continuum. Over time, our learners are asked to draw pictures, form letters, and string letters together to form words, and words to form sentences which they will read or write. Authentic challenges provide the purposeful and authentic reasons to symbolically represent how our children think and feel. Therefore, decoding and encoding written language requires symbolization or assigning meaning to words that are written down. Strategy Three, make reading and writing authentic, for our learners, builds their ability to explore, uncover, and solve challenges while, at the same time, developing their reading and writing ability.

How can I use literacy skills to support authentic learning experiences? The connection between projects and literacy runs deep and one cannot occur without the other. Our text selections, classroom libraries, and book bins spark solutions, ignite ideas, and generate growth-producing dialogue even at the earliest ages. However, we frequently hear all of the following from teachers who are beginning to explore authentic project-based learning:

◆ I have to teach kids how to read first.
◆ My kids can't read yet, so how can they do a project?
◆ How do I do this and still teach literacy?
◆ When do we use books?
◆ I have no time to teach projects, because I have too many other things to do.

Using a project-based learning approach in our teaching gives us the space to make literacy a central focus in the classroom. We know a child's literacy skills are their anchor for gathering information and doing high quality research. With our best reading and writing strategies embedded in the project, the scaffolds we use guide our learners toward finding answers and improving their solutions. Thus, we don't need to start from scratch; we just need to reframe our approach to literacy.

As you read through this chapter and the featured authentic projects, keep in mind that an established project goal gives our authentic challenge a purpose. Armed with a purpose, our learners attempt to solve a problem. Books are the launching point to bring them into the challenge. From books, our kids immediately use stories and information to visualize, take in, and document their connections. These are the same books they may later use during guided reading to practice fluency, use as mentor texts, do a word study, or identify coherence and cohesion in sentences and paragraphs. To illustrate, let's take a look at a second grade example that launched a challenge from our learners' initiative, while using books to spark deeper inquiry.

Our second grade group of children wanted a class pet. They asked many times what they needed to do to get a class pet. In a review of the upcoming science standards that included Next Generation Standard 2-LS4-1, "Make observations of plants and animals to compare the diversity of life in different habitats," an idea for a project was sparked for our kids to earn the privilege of having a class pet. The challenge included the science standards as our learners identified, demonstrated, and created a solution for how they would care for a class pet. As we saw the connections between the authenticity and relevance of the challenge, we mapped them to the required science standards. Our learners needed to demonstrate their ability to classify animals, identify and understand habitats, and observe animals for an authentic reason. To embed literacy within the science class, the ELA standards included: determine the main idea of a text, recount key details and explain how they support the main idea, write opinion pieces on topics or texts, and support a point of view with reasons. After we determined the standards and identified the main learning targets for the project, the challenge came to life: "How can we create the perfect habitat for a pet to thrive in our classroom?"

Let's review how this challenge specifically focused on literacy, as well as connected to improving the fluency and comprehension of our struggling readers. On day one, after morning meeting and word work, we introduced the challenge in our reader's workshop by reading the book *Katie and the Class Pet*, by Fran Manushkin. We posed the question, "How can we create the perfect habitat for a pet to thrive in our classroom?" and asked our kids what they needed to find out in order to answer the question. During our reader's workshop, we had them write the question in a bubble map and independently fill in their bubbles. We required the use of complete sentences as a focus on grammar. Since we only had 40 minutes and other items on our agenda that was all the time we devoted to the project on the first day. On day two, during science and social studies, our learners worked in table groups to compare and contrast the questions they had listed in their bubble maps from day one's activity. Next, the table groups chose their top three questions to share out as a group. We created a list of their items and the class grouped together the similar ones. The grouped items became the research topics they used to guide their work. Day three began with connections to the challenge in our reader's workshop, during guided reading, and during science time. In our reader's workshop, we read Conrad Storad's *Gator, Gator, Second Grader: Classroom Pet or Not?* Our learners focused on sequencing and how the beginning of the story related to the action at the end of it. At the end of the lesson, they discussed the reasons why an alligator would or would not make a good class pet. Later that day, in our writer's workshop time, they created an anchor chart about nonfiction text features. During guided reading, our children read nonfiction texts, such as *Small Pet Care: How to Look After Your Rabbit, Guinea Pig, or Hamster*, by Annabel Blackledge. Later in the day, during science, our learners engaged in "Inference and Information Stations" to use mentor texts, collect data, discover new vocabulary words, and make inferences based on images. Here, they applied the nonfiction text features they had worked with during their writer's workshop to their project. This lasted an additional day or two, in which the inference and information stations included four different tasks. Each station had a specific knowledge capture tool and a scan for vocabulary sheet, which was placed in their interactive science notebook. The first station included nonfiction books with at least ten to twelve nonfiction informational texts of varying levels. The varying levels allowed for differentiation based on the reading levels of each child. The station included books on animals, habitats, and pet care. The children began research on the various topics and used their capture tools to collect data. As they continued their research, they worked through part of the second stage of Finding a Solution. Keep in mind, this was still a time for confusion and ambiguity, as a well-designed challenge comes together at the end of this stage through reflection. If, instead, we find our learners have all the right answers at the beginning of the challenge, we have to go back and revisit the depth of the challenge and our standards.

Take Note: The difference between a high-level PBL challenge and a low-level PBL activity is that our kids must go beyond just finding the information through research. The learner's sum of their literacy skills is to acquire and apply the information to help them create or develop a product. This is based on their evaluations and judgments and is where the real learning occurs. All reading experiences have the potential to become great pre-writing springboards.

An authentic project has to have a purpose and lay out a goal. It is driven by the need to address the challenge. In our class pet example, the reading, research, and writing standards are the engine, but the science standards drive the project. Both content areas address the learning targets. However, the learning targets now have purpose and meaning with a direct connection to the reading and writing through the science research conducted. We built our learners' literacy skills through the science content.

The Common Core State Standards (CCSS), or your specific state standards, have a direct focus on literacy skills. In fact, according to the Common Core State Standards, 70 percent of what learners are to read is nonfiction text. We believe the designers of the standards engineered them in this way for a very specific purpose: to push educators into a space in which literacy takes more of a priority. While it may seem premature, most adults use nonfiction texts in the workplace on a daily basis. Therefore, our learners must be adept at reading and understanding informational texts. Of course, this does not mean that fiction takes a back seat. Rather, it creates a realm in which our fiction texts are a new way to look at core content in other disciplines. Teachers at the Pre-K–third grade levels are fortunate, as we generally have schedules that permit us to develop and design work that integrates all content areas if and when we wish.

We compiled a variety of possible authentic learning experiences aligned to the CCSS in Chapter 2. Refer back to Table 2.3 and challenge yourself to make more direct literacy connections to the examples provided. After trying this on your own, compare your ideas to ours. In Table 4.1, we list possible extensions for several of those projects. You will also gain additional ideas and insight to add to our sample list as you explore the more detailed, day-to-day literacy connections discussed in this chapter's section on Finding a Solution. Please note, for simplification purposes, that we have only provided one CCSS with each example. Other standards apply. Specifically, the writing standards related to "research to build knowledge" are included, but are not listed below. Additionally, as the standards are vertically aligned, the higher the grade level, the more complex the standard is written.

We spent a lot of time looking at how to map our standards to our authentic learning experience. In fact, all of Chapter 2 was dedicated to this. We would be remiss, however, if we didn't reiterate the importance of connecting our literacy standards to the challenge. Whether we focus on a science project, a social studies project, a math project, or even a service-learning project, literacy is the glue that binds those contents together. Examine your scope and sequence or year-at-a-glance plan to identify the skills you want to develop throughout the project. Make the reading, writing, listening, and speaking standards the base of your challenge.

TABLE 4.1 Common Core and Pre-K Standards Aligned to Authentic Literacy Projects

CCSS	Authentic Challenge	Literacy Connection
RL.2.3 Describe how characters in a story respond to major events and challenges	Craft a plan to make the school become more sustainable and present it to the administration	• Read *The Lorax, Just a Dream, Mr. Garbage*, or another environmental or sustainability book of your choice • Write an opinion-based plan to incorporate researched and rejected ideas. Include an explanation of the final solution and point of view on how to make the school more sustainable
W.3.1 Write opinion pieces in which they introduce the topic or book they are writing about, state an opinion, and create an organizational structure that lists reasons. Provide reasons that support the opinion. Provide a concluding statement or section	Draft a proposal to save the art or music program for the school	• Read *Brush of the Gods* or *When Stravinsky Met Nijinsky: Two Artists, Their Ballet, and One Extraordinary Riot* • Write a persuasive proposal to convince the school board to save the school program
1.2 PK.A With prompting and support, retell key details of text that support a provided main idea	Curate the school like a museum	• Read, together, *Henri's Scissors* • Kids record the journey of their art piece and how it developed. Those who are ready write simplified versions

With literacy as the foundation of our project, we make better-informed literacy decisions, determine appropriate reading and writing strategies, and resolve how to associate both with the authentic challenge. For example, in first grade, we chose a nonfiction text for our read-aloud that is complex enough for the various reading levels in our class and chose a strategy that is connected to the overall challenge. An appropriate reading strategy choice, such as the modified version of the KWL chart that we know as Reading and Analyzing Nonfiction (RAN) strategy, helps foster dialogue about prior knowledge. It also connects new vocabulary and information, merges new and old information together, and connects both to the project.

Authentic challenges provide our learners with the chance to engage with nonfiction text with a purpose in mind. This is important, because we know that many kids become disengaged with nonfiction. When they hear or read an informational piece that is loaded with unfamiliar academic or content-specific vocabulary, it can be overwhelming. Although the introduction of new vocabulary is highly encouraged, the amount presented needs to be considered and must have an authentic purpose. If we need to stop every two minutes to explain new vocabulary, we compromise the level of comprehension and pleasure for our learners. On the other hand, if we give our learners multiple opportunities to engage with new vocabulary and content, we increase their ability to retain facts, as they are meaningful and connected to a broader purpose.

A connection to high quality reading strategies with a chosen text provides the context needed to make a learner's reading purposeful. When reading is an expression of our kids' life experiences, it furthers their understanding of concepts and develops the connections to help them become better readers. Authentic project-based learning helps us transform reading instruction so it is not just a standard. In turn, reading instruction becomes a tool to foster our learners' natural curiosities, while we create a passion for reading.

All reading experiences are also pre-writing opportunities. Writing, the other component of literacy, is the long-term process that guides our kids to turn their ideas into viable solutions and well-developed stories. Writing is the foundation for every high quality project. Authentic challenges provide our learners with real-world opportunities to write with purpose. Learners who engage in writing for a purpose understand they will use the diverse genres of writing to communicate what they know and how they feel. It is important that our learners have these varied experiences so they understand how writing reflects the need to convey a specific purpose to a targeted audience. Our Pre-K and kindergarten children may need assistance in writing, but don't discount their symbolic representations and their ability to explain their writing. We encourage writing to be used as frequently as possible throughout the project. In fact, if we add writing materials to any of our play centers, our Pre-K kids automatically gravitate toward them. They enjoy the process of writing as part of their play. The writing has a purpose in the play they do. This, then, transfers into writing for a purpose when we ask them to write for an authentic project experience.

Writing also provides the space for our learners to reflect on their learning and to document their troubleshooting and changes over time. Based on the age and ability of the child, this documentation advances from pictures, to sentences, and then paragraphs. These are not only a valuable insight for us to both formatively and summatively assess their learning, but the act of reflection helps our children to progress through the Stages of Finding a Solution. In order for us to support them in this process, we need to dig deeper into the ways in which we scaffold the learning process at each stage, step, and day of the project challenge.

Our writer's workshop is another time of day that is ripe for literacy skill development. We are sure you would agree that the two things children need to do in order to improve their writing are to read more and write more. The old adage is true, practice makes perfect. However, writing in a vacuum does little to improve writing, as our children rarely see a purpose for doing so. An established writer's workshop tasks our learners to brainstorm a list of possible writing ideas. An authentic challenge gives our writers an additional layer of ideas and a direct purpose to write. At the same time, reading exposes our young learners to new styles of writing, new voices, and new forms and genres of writing. Importantly, it exposes our learners to writing that's better than their own. Subsequently, this exposure helps them to see how they can use academic vocabulary to create meaningful and purposeful writing. It lifts the level of language usage and encourages creativity. Writer's workshop provides structure and gives us, as teachers, a way to model good writing for our learners, practice strategies and skills, and use reflection and conferencing to improve our learners' writing. Purposeful writing and repeated exposure during writer's workshop, in K–3, helps our kids to see that their writing has the potential to evoke feelings and persuade others. It gives them a reason to invent imaginary stories and characters and to prepare presentations through written speeches. In Pre-K, over time, a written story can emerge with depth and meaning if our children are allowed to extend their writing and drawing. This is also the perfect time to begin the draft process. Even in Pre-K, we require at least two drafts before the final copy submission.

During your dedicated writing time, there is also an opportunity to build and strengthen the academic vocabulary needed in the challenge. Vocabulary acquisition doesn't just happen during reading time. Gains in vocabulary are what support the increase in fluency and comprehension when our children read. To fully absorb the meaning of academic words, a child needs to actively think about and use the words in multiple contexts. Writing is another opportunity to practice the authentic challenge vocabulary words, as well as any other vocabulary words that are required by our curriculum. Amazing words, rare words, challenge words, sight words, and any others associated with our reading units are easily integrated into the authentic writing that takes place during the project challenge. However, rather than simply remembering a definition of a vocabulary word or memorizing how to spell them for the weekly spelling test, our kids are asked to provide meaning and context to the words through their writing. Whether they draft a proposal to implement change or craft an opinion piece to support their solution, the use of vocabulary words strengthens the required writing. It also provides us with an opportunity to assess their understanding of the vocabulary terms. Through this process, we see our children advance in all areas of literacy. Reading, writing, and conversational speaking skills improve, as the uses of the challenge's academic vocabulary are infused throughout the project.

As our learners progress through an authentic challenge, we map the relevance of the challenge to their critical reading skills and assess their writing to determine their levels of understanding. How does the use of Bloom's Taxonomy levels improve our learners' reading and writing experience during a project? Let's use sight words as an example. What our learners can do with the information they see in print and with what they hear can be very different. A child can point to a word and tell you what word she sees, because she has memorized it. She has gained the knowledge of what the word looks like. Can she define the word? Can she use the word in a sentence? If she were to read the word in a story, would she know its context? These are all reading standards that we must assess to make sure our young readers reach their full potential. These critical skills are easily aligned in an authentic challenge to measure their development over time.

Bloom's Taxonomy supports our quest to embed reading and writing at each of the levels in our authentic challenges. There is a marked difference between applying what we learn and creating or designing a solution to a challenge. The design or creation level encourages our learners to demonstrate their ability to analyze, synthesize, and evaluate information in order to find and create a solution. To just apply a learning target to a lesson certainly helps, in some respects, our learners to become more fluent readers. Except, we want our readers to become lifelong learners who think beyond the text and make meaningful associations between their lives and what they read. Therefore, we need to reach for the highest level of thinking once they comprehend what they have read. In Table 4.2, we identify the difference between mid-level application activities and high-level authentic learning experiences. By designing a project at the highest level you have created a purpose and reason to make reading real. This creates, in real time, more meaningful reading experiences. It also provides opportunities to increase reading fluency and comprehension, vocabulary development, and writing proficiency.

We have spent a good deal of this book looking at how the revised version of Bloom's Taxonomy supports authentic project-based learning. At this point in your journey, you may still separate reading and writing into designated times of the day or maybe you have started to integrate them

TABLE 4.2 Application versus Creation

Application Level Activities	Creation Level Authentic Learning Experiences
How can we investigate the habitats that are all around us?	How can we create the perfect habitat for a class pet to thrive in our classroom? How can we safely move the habitat of an animal in our schoolyard?
How can we prove that shapes are a part of our daily life?	How can we use everyday shapes to improve our school's hallway traffic? How can we use shapes to create art installations for our community?
How can we effectively grow plants?	How can we redesign our school's gardens so our plants have the right environment to grow? How can we help to establish a successful community garden?

into your other content areas. In either case, as you move through Bloom's, you graduate from the planning of application level activities to the design of creation level authentic learning experiences. As the examples in Table 4.2 show, there is a marked difference between these two categories. We know you will still need to ensure your learners can answer the questions listed in the activities column. However, answering the questions at the creation level provides a deeper foundation to support the acquisition and mastery of language that is written, spoken, and read. Refer to Table 4.3 for examples of how to align your approach to literacy to Bloom's.

We ended the second paragraph of this chapter with questions we know many of you have. We understand you are concerned about how to teach literacy through project-based learning. That is one of the reasons why you are reading this book. We also know that many of you

TABLE 4.3 Bloom's Alignment to Literacy

Bloom's Taxonomy	Reading	Writing and Speaking
Creating	1 Rewrite the ending to a story related to the challenge topic 2 Read and research a variety of cultures to create a cultural awareness event designed to raise funds for the library's cultural books section	1 Final individual written piece (narrative or expository) 2 Final group presentation
Evaluating	1 Extend reading and information to build our new ideas 2 Compare sources to determine similarities	1 Reflect on the results of prototype testing 2 Plan out next steps to work toward a final solution using a storyboard format

Analyzing	1 Continuously read stories and analyze sections using the "zoom in" strategy to increase and extend vocabulary word base 2 Determine the author's point of view as it relates to the challenge	1 Use of writer's notebook with responses that integrate new vocabulary words 2 Integrate new knowledge with the project challenge criteria through verbal or written responses
Applying	1 Answer pre/post-reading questions related to the processing of new information and making personal connections 2 Engage in hands-on activities, experiments, and labs that guide learners to connect and apply project vocabulary and information they have read	1 Write out and describe the steps on how to create their final products using the writing process that is developmentally appropriate for the learner's age 2 Write questions for and conduct an interview of an expert on the topic challenge
Understanding	1 Classify research books into appropriate categories 2 Use mentor texts to model good reading and writing habits	1 Write sentences and put sentence strips in correct order, using vocabulary words or context clues, identify beginning, middle, and end of stories 2 Restate the challenge in their own words in journals or a writer's notebook
Remembering	1 Reading response and reflection discussions 2 Vocabulary development through varied, rich project related texts	1 Vocabulary development and definitions 2 Prepare a "What I Learned" presentation

are wondering what this looks like in your classrooms. As you move into this next section on how literacy supports each Stage of Finding a Solution, think of it in the same way as you approach a lesson plan. Each day is teased out to provide activities that support literacy development. Remember, do what is right for you and your kids. Please note that the examples we have provided do not include field studies, outdoor observations, school walks and tours, field trips and other hands-on experiences. Each challenge will look slightly different and may need to incorporate a bit more than we have written or you may need to skip a few things that we have included. This is just a sample to help you think about your project from a literacy perspective. Also, don't forget about the formative assessment of each stage, as you incorporate literacy. Chapter 5 is dedicated to maximizing formative assessment in authentic project-based learning experiences.

Literacy in Stage 1 of Finding a Solution

> ### Authentic Challenge and Purpose
>
> How do we know if our kids understand the challenge and why they are doing it?
>
> 2 to 3 days

Day One of Stage 1

At the start of our project, literacy skills are either introduced or practiced. When we introduce the challenge to our kids, they think about what the project is about and why they are doing it. This is, from a literacy standard perspective, the main idea and the purpose of the challenge. Here, after our kids have thought about the challenge, we use notecards, paper, or single bubble maps to have them draw or write the key details they already know and want to know (KWL). This provides an opportunity for our learners to shed light on their prior knowledge, as they identify key details. Your focus is on the progression of inquiry. As your kids begin the project process, you will experience lots of blank stares and many "huh" or "what" moments. Since this is the start of the inquiry process, it is expected. We don't have to fill the silence by teaching them. We want them to simmer in ambiguity and experience the struggle between not knowing and using prior knowledge to start generating ideas. If the wait time goes on for too long without a significant response, we simply repeat the challenge narrative and have our kids turn and talk to each other for support. They are used to the adult in the room explaining the answers, so they may be waiting for just that to happen. This is our chance to create space for learner-centered inquiry.

Days Two and Three of Stage 1

We begin our reader's workshop with a nonfiction or fiction text and choose a literacy standard as our focus. Our choice is a reflection of what we want to do before, during, and after we read the text. Will we focus on the rare or wow vocabulary in the story? Will we focus on main ideas and key details? After reading the text, we create a main idea anchor chart. Now, we have a perfect segue to connect the text to the project and reflect on our kids' KWL activity from day one. Next, we create a class circle map to define the challenge. Then we organize them into what our learners' interests are about the challenge and what they want to know more about. It is the perfect time to "add-on" to the kids' KWL chart and to have them write their own "what I want to learn more about." This direct reading and thinking strategy is a pre-reading activity that gives our learners the opportunity to preview a chunk of text, make predictions, and then read to confirm or adjust their predictions. This continues until a whole text is read. Once the text is read, we go back and connect their work to the original KWL chart and make any necessary additions to it.

During centers, our learners practice summarizing a narrative text. We have to be sure to relate this narrative text to the challenge, as it is an excellent way to begin to build your project-related vocabulary. The words can later be added to a classroom vocabulary word wall. This is also the perfect opportunity to include our project vocabulary as weekly spelling or challenge words.

Literacy in Stage 2 of Finding a Solution

Information and Prototyping
How do we know if our kids have created a viable product?
3 to 8 days

Day One of Stage 2

Now that our learners know the purpose of their challenge, it is time to research and gather information. They have determined what information they already know and identified the questions for which they need to find the answers. Since research takes many forms, it can take shape both inside and outside of the classroom. Whether or not our kids work on the challenge in groups or individually, we recommend that each child do individual research and document their own information. This helps with the formative assessment we discuss in Chapter 5. Here, literacy and information stations are an excellent way to incorporate multiple literacy standards and various concepts maps to capture their thinking. These include the use of numerous text features, description of key details, identification of words and phrases, and recognition of the parts of a story. Literacy and information stations include the following four areas:

1   A **fiction station** that has a fiction text focused on plot and setting or character. We usually see the teacher reading the text in this station. In some cases, teachers use this station as part of their guided reading.

2   An **inference card station** that has at least four images related to the project. Our kids draw out information about the challenge based on the visual cues from these cards. This is a great activity for our visual learners.

3   A **nonfiction station** that includes ten to twelve nonfiction books. These books relate to the challenge and include a variety of reading levels. This allows for differentiation to meet the needs of all of our learners.

4   A **writing station** where learners express their opinions about the project vocabulary words or the purpose of the project. This can be completed as drawings or with words. Older children begin to classify the materials they may want to use or tech tools they would like to incorporate. Younger learners describe the sensory experience and how it relates to the project challenge.

In the first few days a project challenge takes up 30 to 40 minutes each day. It is important to visually connect and reiterate that all of their research leads to the development of the final product. It may take up our entire reader's workshop and science time. After the first few days, we will not always devote the entire class period to the project. Where it is appropriate in our schedule, we make room for word study, guided reading, and independent reading. Writer's workshop provides relevant writing ideas that lead to personal stories and take them through the writing process. Each day, a few minutes before or after a transition or before engaging in their project time, we may have our learners journal about their plans or project experience before they gather as group. We choose a certain number of journal entries to randomly share before work time starts.

Days Two and Three of Stage 2

By now, our learners have had a chance to start their research by going through the literacy and information stations. Keep in mind, with these stations we have discovered that one day just scratches the surface. Our learners barely have time to draw pictures or write their new vocabulary down. Some may have just finished correctly gluing their interactive notebooks. Thus, based on our observations, we may need to extend the number of days, as needed. We are also prepared with a list of questions that promote thinking. We create anchor charts that help us to remember the questions we want to ask our kids. Is your research connected to the challenge? Have you found enough information? How could you check that the information you have collected is right? Have we left out any information that is important? We spend as much time as is necessary to ensure our learners can answer these questions and complete the literacy and information stations we described in day one of Stage 2:

1   Fiction station
2   Inference card station
3   Nonfiction station
4   Writing station

Day Four of Stage 2

Here is our first opportunity to debrief the stations, do group check-ins, and assess research results. We reflect on whether or not our kids have gathered accurate data at their individual reading levels. This takes place where it fits most naturally in our daily schedule. We think about our morning activities, reader's workshop time, or another designated time during our day that works for us. We might do a mini-lesson on fiction versus nonfiction, create a class anchor chart, and then sort and classify the books from the learning stations or in our class library. A mini-lesson on inferences and review of the four inference cards from our inference card station are also great activities to support our learners at this stage. We take the time to review new project vocabulary words during guided reading and centers. Here, we have seen some teachers take their learners' original KWL chart and add what they learned to the chart or to the buckets that we discuss in Chapter 5. Now is also a good time to assess understanding through "just right" book choices. We do this as a review of personal reading inventories to add new books or adjust the "just right" book choices they've made. The reading choices now have a purpose, because their books are related to the challenge they are trying to solve or understand. Their book bins may contain books that relate to the challenge, but are not directly connected to it. This might include a story about being a good teammate, kids taking risks, or making things for a reason.

Day Five of Stage 2

This is the day for project teams to come together and share their information and start to brainstorm ideas about their first prototype. We review the traits of a good teammate with mentor texts or read-alouds during morning meeting or at another convenient point during our day. This is also a time where we introduce a team contract for first grade through third grade. At this point, we begin to see our learners transition to the application level with their information. Here is where we facilitate critical thinking by asking targeted questions related to accurate data, data comparisons, and research of nonfiction texts. During this time, our children move from understanding the purpose of the project to the application of the information they have gathered in order to draw their initial conclusions. We don't want to forget to strongly encourage our children to use their new vocabulary words. In support, we provide thinking maps, visuals, and prototype formula sheets that have the vocabulary we want them to use. We are also prepared with a series of questions related to the purpose of the challenge:

Why are you collecting this information?

How did you reach this conclusion?

Does your conclusion match the information you collected?

Our learners will not have all of the needed information or the correct prototypes at this point, but they will be their original thoughts. It is those original thoughts that they will mold and develop as a team. As we progress through the challenge together, they will add more information based on the books they read, the questions we ask, experiments we stage, and their personal experiences. The use of the Pass Around or Retell strategy encourages our learners to share information collected, discuss the results, and add to their learning. It is an excellent writing activity, both in pictures and in words, for our learners to focus on writing as a process that promotes peer conferencing. This layering helps them to uncover the changes and additions they may want to make throughout the troubleshooting process.

Day Six of Stage 2

Now is the time to incorporate independent reading through our reader's workshop. Book-bin choice reading supports their growth and understanding of the targeted content. Dedicated time for groups to work on designing their first prototype is also scheduled on this day. To maximize our support of our learners and efficiently schedule our day, we plan to meet with guided reading groups while other groups are building their prototypes. Here, we choose our preferred reading strategies to help our learners refer back to their research and the project challenge as they begin to draw their first conclusions. This is a pivotal stage, as our kids automatically draw conclusions when we consistently tie our classroom work to the challenge. This is where they begin to think about what their final product might look like. It is the perfect time for our learners to apply their initial understanding of content to their first prototype design. Kids will have outlandish first prototypes and want to add unrealistic options. Let them! We want our learners to go this far and applaud their first draft. We need to encourage them to own their first draft. This ownership is part of the intrinsic motivation we discuss in Chapter 6. As we implement authentic project-based experiences, we find the learning process of going through each stage gives our children multiple opportunities to refine their prototype. The key is that they use their own initial design from the beginning. While it can be hard at times, we don't want to lead them into a predetermined outcome and must be careful to continually encourage and foster their curiosity. When they read more books, do experiments, and engage with writing aligned to the content, they naturally see changes they want to make.

Day Seven of Stage 2

In our experience, it usually takes groups one to two days to complete their first prototype. During our reader's workshop, if possible, our book choices and guided reading are related to the project. If this is not possible, we create and add a few questions that help our learners connect their project to the reading we are doing at the time. Throughout the project process, many of our teachers connect and use Daily Five literature circles, author's perspective, and reader's notebooks. This simultaneously helps to support the connection to our literacy strategies and provides additional ideas on how to troubleshoot the prototype. Most importantly, it also keeps the reading authentic for our learners. At this juncture, an effective way to assess the progress of our teams and our learners' thinking is to have them use their writing skills to document their plans and conversations, and to take notes in an interactive journal.

Day Eight of Stage 2

As we draw to the close of Stage 2, we schedule a chunk of time to work on the feedback process. This is so important for improving prototypes that we cannot afford to skip it. Opportunities to present prototypes can take many different forms. Try a class gallery walk, schedule team partner shares, or pick another presentation method of choice. Examples of this might include a silent museum tour around the room, cooperative learning structures such as carousel feedback, inside and outside circles, and the one stray activity. We have our learners express in in their journals or draw pictures about how they felt when they were able to give and receive feedback. In any case, feedback is the key to close out this stage. Our learners take this feedback and use the new ideas to launch into the next phase.

Literacy in Stage 3 of Finding a Solution

Perspective and Point of View

How do we know if our kids have thought about different ideas?

2 to 4 days

Day One of Stage 3

Stage 3 is the perfect time to use fiction to ferret out the author's purpose and main idea, much in the same way we want our learners to identify the purpose and main idea of the challenge. They reflect on their work using the same "author's purpose" standard (CCSS RI 3.6) in which they need to be able to distinguish their point of view from the author's point of view. Here, we have listed some sample questions to stimulate the thinking our kids do:

What other points of view are out there?

What if you were to pretend you were someone else?

How would you feel or what would you think from another person, place, or thing's perspective?

This is the perfect place for you to read a book that explores point of view and perspective. Drew Daywalt's *The Day the Crayons Quit* is an excellent book for looking at perspective and one that we use to model this standard for our learners. We do a read-aloud of the book and then have our kids work independently to explore each crayon's letter and unique point of view. We use a graphic organizer as a tool to capture their thinking. Another choice of reading might be *I am the Dog, I am the Cat* by Donald Hall. Since many children have pets, they can make text-to-self connections. The book has two voices and two perspectives within the same text.

Day Two of Stage 3

Whether our focus is to read fiction or nonfiction, our role is to support our readers as they make meaning within and beyond the literature and genres they read. We create the time and space, as teachers, to make sure they deepen their understanding of main idea and point of view. We utilize this time to strengthen our learners' personal perspective and the audience's point of view through the use of both narrative and expository texts. During this stage, our learners benefit from explicit instruction in how to activate prior knowledge, make predictions, identify particular structures in stories, use graphic organizers, and ask and answer questions. We like to use the "I say, you say" and retell writing activities to help us complete this portion of Stage 3. These help our early learners distinguish first person perspective and, for second and third grade, the third person. The T-notes strategy is a capture tool that enables our learners to demonstrate their understanding of the texts they are reading. They can be created for our Pre-K learners where we chart their responses. For this, we create a two-column chart with the left side labeled as main ideas and the right side labeled as details and examples. Our learners then complete the chart during their reading time. After reading, they review their notes and, as a class, look for connections to the challenge.

Day Three of Stage 3

Teacher read-alouds are the entry points to introduce and practice critical reading strategies. They are especially important for our children who have not had much exposure to reading. The read-alouds provide opportunities for our learners to hear project vocabulary in action, hear fluent reading, and increase their background knowledge of the challenge's content. Therefore, we connect our concept talk and discussions to our read-alouds and project. These text discussions help our learners move beyond the story to make associations with the authentic challenge. We continue to use our mentor texts to explore points of view and any other reading strategies on which we are focused at our school or for our district. An example of this in action would be to read *The True Story of the Three Little Pigs*, *The Wolf's Story*, and *The Pea and the Princess* in conjunction with one another. These books are written from the opposite perspective of the traditional fairy tales and help our kids understand different points of view. From this, in our writer's workshop, our learners create a partner's perspective poem in pairs to continue an analysis of point of view. Then, they connect their poems to the authentic challenge.

This provides us with insight into our learners' personal perspectives, as a point of view can be sparked by their memories or experiences connected to visuals or photographs. Throughout the project, we continue to explicitly create moments where we connect our discussions back to the authentic challenge.

Day Four of Stage 3

Our learners engage in investigative reading activities, reciprocal reading, and close reading strategies. Specifically, close reading works well here, as it requires our learners to determine the purpose of the text and the author's point of view. This is done without any of the usual front-loading teachers often do before reading. This reading strategy not only helps our learners understand complex text, but also aids them in their cognitive approach to point of view, when they independently read a similar book. For the challenge, our kids need to consider the intended audience's point of view. The use of close reading with fiction and nonfiction texts, to spur conversations around the authentic challenge, helps our learners use their knowledge and understanding to decide upon their personal point of view. An added benefit ensures they have looked at their solution through a variety of others' points of view.

Literacy in Stage 4 of Finding a Solution

> ### Actions and Consequences
>
> How do we know if our kids have moved beyond their initial beliefs?
>
> 2 to 4 days

Day One of Stage 4

By this stage, our learners have decided upon their point of view. We use stories, activities, and questioning strategies to make sure our learners understand their final product has both positive and negative impacts on people, places, and things. Role plays, scenarios, and dramatic play activities all provide opportunities for our children to make inferences and predictions about their solutions. Reading strategies help our learners articulate what consequences their product will have on others. Here, we utilize dialogue and debate to demonstrate the relevant and important connections our kids have made with the people, places, and things their solution will impact. A SWOT analysis works well to accomplish our goals at this stage. You may be familiar with it as a strengths, weaknesses, opportunity, and threats protocol. In our Chapter 5 discussion, we use the simplified terms for our younger learners: Good, Grow, Possible, and Buggy. During this analysis, our learners put themselves in the role of the audience. They give feedback based on their own experiences and work to provide feedback on the implications of their final product.

Day Two of Stage 4

To begin a non-traditional conversation, our learners communicate with us via dialogue journals. The discussion starts with prompts we provide for our learners. For our early writers, we engage in a shared writing activity with them where we hold the pen to guide their formation of the words. Our assessment requires us to read their initial response to the prompt and then answer it. This process continues in a back and forth manner over the course of this stage. Our learners' responses open a window to where and in what ways they have made changes in their beliefs and ideas. Even young children, from the ages of 3 to 6, have the ability to make thoughtful decisions about behaviors and keen observations about changes in their environment. Our younger learners have the ability to devise simple solutions where they express their intentions and reactions with gestures, drawings and limited, yet emerging, vocabularies. Our older learners have the capability of writing multipart, sequenced solutions enriched by their layered experiences, reflections, and predictions. Moving through this process ensures the development of new vocabulary, reading skills, and writing skills as our learners plan and reflect on a daily basis. Here, they truly begin to develop the linguistic and conceptual structures that guide them to formulate and share their complex thoughts.

Day Three of Stage 4

As we continue to implement writing as a reflection tool, we encourage you to try new strategies that help our kids see additional points of view. The use of SCAMPER (substitute, combine, adapt, modify, put to another use, eliminate, and reverse) teaches our kids to better view how ideas are alike, different, and relatable. The SCAMPER tool is used in a variety of ways and we encourage you to choose what works best for you and your class, small group of learners, or an individual child. You can choose one letter from SCAMPER and have all your children use it to provide either verbal or written feedback. You can spread the letters out over the whole day and kids can take their time and independently respond to them. You can set it up for teams to create collaborative feedback that they generate together. You can also use the example question stems developed by Mind Tools and hand them out for your early readers.

It is still important to continue to deepen our learners' reading comprehension abilities, so don't lose sight of this. In fact, today is a good opportunity to use compare and contrast texts to activate and extend our learners' background knowledge and enrich their academic vocabulary. It is also the perfect opportunity to try mental imagery journaling with our kids. To do this, we have our kids picture themselves planning for their presentation of their solution to the challenge. What they envision is what they should reflect about in their mental imagery journal entry.

Day Four of Stage 4

It is time to focus on having our learners polish their written pieces. The use of what we call a "To Be or Not to Be Protocol" is appropriate here. For this, we have our kids partner up with a peer. In the partnership, we start with one child who explains his or her biggest problem with their identified solution. Their partner provides suggestions for improvement. During this conversation, the partners take notes, if they are capable. Then, the partners switch to run through the protocol again. Don't stop here, however. To truly have our learners process the feedback, they need to formally reflect. To do this, we have each child sit alone, with their notes, and write down each suggestion. For each suggestion, they list a pro and a con of implementing the suggestion. Older grades are welcome to implement this protocol in small groups rather than just as partners.

Since our kids are nearing the end of Stage 4, we want to continue to provide them with options to enhance their solutions. We add new books, rearrange reading bins, and engage in small book studies with various teams' members. We also continue to model, teach, and promote our various literacy strategies to increase the levels of reading proficiency. Good readers use a range of strategies before, during, and after reading, so we need to continue to support the growth of our kids, even as we advocate for their own use of self-monitoring checks.

Literacy in Stage 5 of Finding a Solution

> ### Evaluations and Conclusions
>
> How do we know if our kids have reached the best possible solution for their audience?
>
> 2 to 3 days

Day One of Stage 5

As you enter this stage, you have completed a lot of good work to support your learners! At multiple points throughout the project, you have:

◆ created a text-rich environment;
◆ guided your class through locating and organizing information from various sources;
◆ used diverse fiction and nonfiction books to help your learners draw conclusions;
◆ taught reading as a process of making meaning;
◆ taught the elements of words, sentences affixes, prefixes, and other components;
◆ designed tasks that help learners to use their thinking skills in multiple situations;
◆ provided opportunities for speaking, listening, and writing;
◆ read various materials and texts with your learners for comprehension and critical analysis.

Our final stage is to have our learners evaluate their final product one last time to ensure it meets the needs of the original challenge and its intended audience. On this day, we want our kids to review the presentation rubric. There are many rubrics on the web that you can adapt, you might already have a school or a district rubric, or, if you think your kids are up to it, have them actually co-develop a rubric with you. Once we have reviewed the rubric with our learners, there is the option to role-play possible presentation scenarios with them. With older children, we also like to have them watch a presentation and provide feedback on it. In either case, we provide our learners with a firm grasp of what a good presentation is supposed to include. We find, however, that the more presentations our learners participate in, the better they get at them.

If our project does not include the need for a presentation, we utilize this day to make any additional adjustments to their writing pieces. This is a good time to bring in upper grade levels for support. We have had great success pairing an eleventh grade ELA class with our own. If your elementary and secondary schools are located close enough together, a mini-field trip to one building or the other works. Otherwise, a virtual exchange will suffice. Our learners are then able to take the feedback to make any final edits.

Day Two of Stage 5

Now is the time to actually start presentation practice. We make sure our kids review the presentation rubric one final time. During the presentation practice, peers use the rubrics to provide feedback. We also make the time to take a video of the practice sessions. Then, we have our kids watch the video to note any idiosyncratic movements they may be prone to making. Today is also a good time to introduce project summary maps. For this, we have our learners either review a chosen text, related to the challenge, or use their journals to actually create a story. This story must include the main characters, the problems they face, and the solutions to the problem. This summary map is designed to help our learners note any gaps that may exist in their final products. If time remains, and our children need it, we have them work on their final writing pieces. If any additional writing edits still need to happen, we set aside time for this. Finally, we have our learners complete a team reflection, in their own words.

Day Three of Stage 5

The presentation day is finally here! We make sure our expert audience has the presentation rubric, in advance of the actual presentation. We review it with them and answer any questions they may have. Keep in mind that these experts are not responsible for providing the actual grade or skills check-off for our kids. However, we do want our learners to reflect on the rubric feedback from these experts. Once the presentation is complete, our learners are excited to discuss the results of the presentation. A whole class discussion is appropriate, but we also like to have our kids do a silent, written reflection, as well. Our Pre-K kids might like to draw a picture to represent their presentation and their perceived outcome of it. Finally, we take the time to celebrate the end of the challenge. This is a moment our learners will remember for years to come, so we encourage them to bask in their success.

When you think about it, it is almost impossible to separate literacy from any of the work that we do in the classroom. From social studies to science, reading and writing are foundational components to understand the concepts of citizenship and nature. Even in math, we have moved to a space in which we ask our learners to reason, rather than memorize. It is through this reasoning that we call upon our children to write out explanations or decipher word problems. Even in our specials, such as art and music, literacy plays a central role. The ability to read music or decode the meaning of an art piece requires us to embed the core skills that we build through literacy lessons. Thus, developing authentic, project-based challenges steeped in literacy not only supports skills development, but produces lifelong readers, writers, and problem-solvers. Strategy Three, make reading and writing authentic, furthermore develops our children as lifelong learners who appreciate their reading and writing skills as a means for communicating their thoughts, conclusions, and point of view, but also piques their natural curiosity as learners. What are your next steps? Reflect here, before you move onto the following chapter, on how you will make reading and writing authentic.

Where are You?
What are You Thinking?
How do You Feel?

Take Action	Seek Community	Think Aloud
Choose a literacy unit that you already teach. Determine two or three possible ways in which you could embed that unit into the authentic challenge. Develop this literacy connection into the project challenge you've been designing since Chapter 1.	Share your findings with a teaching partner or curriculum coach. Determine the areas in which you can deepen the literacy connection or add another literacy connection within the challenge. How can these literacy additions strengthen your learners' solutions?	After reading this chapter, reflect on how your current literacy lessons and approach can be shifted by designing authentic challenges. Predict how your readers and writers will now be able to make connections between content areas.

5

Strategy Four: Maximize Formative Assessments in Your Project

How do I maximize my use of formative assessment to set my learners up for success?

You've spent the first half of this book thinking about how to develop your authentic challenge. The design process may or may not have felt new to you. As we move forward, we want you to think about the basic assessment tools you already use in your classroom. Thinking maps, exit slips, journal entries, quizzes, running records, and interactive notebooks are all tools that are more than likely familiar to your kids. This premise of formative assessment remains the same as we design projects for our class. Strategy Four is to maximize our use of formative assessments throughout the project to monitor our learners as they master the standards throughout each Stage of Finding a Solution.

How do I maximize my use of formative assessment to set my learners up for success? As we discussed in Chapter 2, our authentic challenge is derived from the standards and their connection to the real world. This strategy gives us the opportunity to connect our learners' prior knowledge to their impact on their present world. As they foreshadow how the future may look, they are able to innovate and design solutions based on what they already know. This ensures the action of linking a real-world challenge to what is relevant to our learners, as we pique their natural curiosity. We would be remiss, however, if we did not continually assess our learners. Therefore, it is important to consider these questions related to various portions of the project process:

1   As children complete research at the beginning of a project, in what ways will you assess the quality, quantity, and accuracy of their research?

2   As kids design a prototype, how will you assess their attention to detail, their ability to troubleshoot various design flaws, and its connection to the design challenge?

3   As learners propose a solution, how will you assess their ability to make a change or improve their work based on feedback from peers, experts, and you?

The formative assessments we choose to use throughout the project need to be authentic to the challenge. Let's use the example from Chapter 2 where we challenged our third graders to increase funding for the art or music program at school. At this grade level, many state tests require an assessment for both informational and opinion writing pieces. We want our learners to be prepared for this test and to do so in an effective and meaningful way that is authentic to them. This example provides a great opportunity to infuse writing for a purpose and an audience outside of the classroom. To support the reasons why a music or art program is important to the development of critical thinking skills, based on research conducted, our learners support their justification for the need to increase funding. Additionally, they have the opportunity to express their own opinions, based on the informational research conducted. These writing pieces are easily embedded during a writer's or reader's workshop. In order for this final writing piece to be ready for the intended audience, it needs to go through all the phases of the writing process. An opportunity to pre-write, draft, peer review, and revise are all formative assessment points that improve the published product. A variety of formative assessment tools that strengthen a final product, including this one, are included in Table 5.1.

We want to ensure our learners demonstrate what they know and what they can do with the standards. These are the critical stages at which we want to design assessments for their thinking. To teach and assess critical thinking within the authentic learning experience or project we want to implement multiple opportunities for formative checks. These include both formal and informal opportunities to check for

TABLE 5.1 Stages of Finding a Solution through Formative Assessment

Stages of Finding a Solution	Indicators of Growth and Mastery With prompting and support …	Possible Formative Assessments and Opportunities to Measure Growth
Stage 1: Authentic Challenge and Purpose How do we know if our kids understand the challenge and why they are doing it?	• Document awareness of their clearly defined role • Articulate the purpose of the challenge—they can say why they are doing the project • Identify the final requirements or products and connect them to the purpose of the project	• Space Method • GRASP • Knowledge Tree Guides • Think-Pair-Share • Co-op Strip Paragraphs • KWL Chart • Reframing Matrix • Single Bubble Chart
Stage 2: Information and Prototyping How do we know if our kids have created a viable product?	• Gather accurate information through hands-on activities, reading, and read-alouds • Involve them in experiences that ask them to apply the data • Participate in several iterations of a final product with all kids/groups completing at least two drafts	• Knowledge Inventories • 3-2-1 Reflection • Open-Narrow-Close • Interactive Journal • I Know/You Know • Storyboarding • Quiz-Quiz-Trade • 3-12-3 Brainstorm
Stage 3: Perspective and Point of View How do we know if our kids have thought about different ideas?	• Engage in opportunities to interact with experts • Listen to and evaluate the opinions of their peers • Change their perspective throughout the project process that is reflective of their growth	• Guided Reciprocal Peer Questioning • Roving Reporter • Author Study • Anchor Charts • Role Play • Scenarios • Flow Maps • Double Bubble Maps
Stage 4: Actions and Consequences How do we know if our kids have moved beyond their initial beliefs?	• Document their possible solutions at multiple points during the project process • Share the consequences of their design and identified possible changes • Discuss ideas and justify when and how to make changes	• Think it Through • Experts "In the House" • SCAMPER • Pyramid Teaching • Learning Logs • Consequence and Sequel • See Think Wonder • Multi-Flow Map
Stage 5: Considerations and Conclusions How do we know if our kids have reached the best possible solution for their audience?	• Weigh possible solutions to the challenge • Articulate why some possible solutions would not work • Determine their final solutions	• Café Conversations • Reflective Central Idea Diagram • SWOT Analysis (Good, Grow, Possible, Buggy) • Spider Web Discussion • Socratic Seminar • Mind Maps • Brace Maps/Fishbone • Text Clue Conclusion Groups

understanding and mastery. The results are then used to inform our instruction for individuals, small groups, and/or our entire class.

Formative assessment and grading practices vary from school to school and district to district. In many contexts, we are required to take grades throughout the marking period. Grades give parents insight into their child's ability to demonstrate their understanding and application of standards. The use of formative assessments are viable as grades and can be used to provide evidence of a learner's progress, for both report cards and parent communication. It is also a way for us to tangibly chart the progress of our learners in order to make informed decisions about the next steps in each child's learning plan.

We formatively assess our learners' thinking around the standards, identifiable skills, and their own thinking about the content at each Stage of Finding a Solution. Each stage has a clear indicator of growth and/or mastery. These indicators are our keys to knowing when and if our learners are prepared to move forward in the project process.

The types of formative assessments we choose need to be aligned to the kind of thinking intended. Table 5.1 is a list of the possible formative assessments that you might choose to do at each Stage of Finding a Solution. We have identified and aligned these formative assessments to match the types of critical thinking necessary for mastery throughout the project. These tools are used by project-based learning educators with whom we have worked from around the world. Just remember, what works for one learner, may not be the best for another. Thus, vary your approach and tools at each Stage of Finding a Solution to ensure you meet the needs of all your learners.

Stage 1: Authentic Challenge and Purpose

> How do we know if our kids understand the challenge and why they are doing it?

The start of an authentic project signals the beginning of the questioning journey that leads to our learners Finding a Solution. After we give our learners their challenge, rather than beginning with a traditional pre-assessment of content knowledge, we provide our learners with an opportunity to systematically embark on their exploration of the given challenge. They do this as they ask questions. These questions are also known as the inquiry process, as they lead to more questions. Figure 5.1 provides an overview of example general questions that may arise.

Figure 5.1 Sample Inquiry Process Questions

Possible Inquiry Questions
What kind of challenge is this? What are we trying to accomplish? Why is it important that we do this project? What information do we already have? Who might help us as experts? How will this impact our community?

We use a KWL or a single bubble chart when we introduce or set up the project challenge for our kids. We have our learners do a think-pair-share with the questions they have about the challenge. The charts might be a shared writing activity in Pre-K and early kindergarten and move to more individual, learner-led questions, as they get older. This encourages them to seek out, share with, draw, and write about the information needed to begin the project. Simultaneously, this helps us, based on their prior knowledge, to determine at which level of Bloom's Taxonomy they need to begin or enter into the project (see Table 5.2 on page 91). This also sparks the discovery we mentioned in Chapter 3. It sets the tone and paves the way for continued critical thinking throughout the project.

Rather than beginning a project by simply announcing its start, we want to formally invite our learners into the project challenge. This gives them the first opportunity to ask questions. We want to grab the attention of our kids and begin this process of inquiry. While there are many ways to invite children into the learning process, we prefer to not only engage them, but develop and honor their natural curiosity and excitement to explore. This is the moment that sets our kids off on their project journey and gets them to ask important questions.

Don't be scared of the ambiguity when there are no questions at first. It takes time for our learners to settle into the rhythm of asking questions. We certainly have to model it for them and push them to deeper questions through our own questioning of them. However, we know we have hit the nail on the head when our learners give us a blank stare and ask, "huh?" Often, they then look at each other and say, "What are we supposed to do?" We let them simmer here for a while. We have to resist the urge to give them the answers. We use wait time, questioning strategies, and restate the challenge, if necessary, for our learners. We ask what words they know and what words they don't know. We then add these unknown words to the items they need to learn and define.

It is also important to remember that our learners may be frustrated when there is no immediate answer to the challenge. This is key, as they are only in the first of the Five Stages of Finding a Solution.

> **Take Note:** In the beginning, our learners should not be able to answer the question or challenge we pose. In fact, in many early childhood rooms, for up to the first three days, our learners will look at us with that blank stare, say "huh?" and start off with no questions at all. While our instinct is to teach them everything they need to answer the question or challenge, our role is to get them to ask questions through the project introduction. This means we need to provide our learners with the scaffolds and tools to begin to generate questions.

To illustrate our point, let's revisit, in more detail, our Chapter 3 example of the kindergarten weather unit we turned into an authentic challenge. To introduce the weather unit, we brought in a local fireman. He asked our kids what kinds of scary weather they had experienced and if they had experienced any other frightening events related to weather, such as power outages and downed trees. The fireman explained that they get called out for many weather-related emergencies. During these calls, they find many people are unprepared for these emergencies. Thus, the fireman challenged our kids to create a natural disaster and weather survival kit and evacuation plan for their home. Once the fireman left, our kids were given a single bubble map to write or draw the questions they had about what the fireman asked them to do. They wrote questions and/or drew silently for five minutes. Next, they buddied up with a shoulder or table partner to share their questions and pictures. They then did a whole class share out of their questions.

During sessions similar to this, our role as a facilitator can take on various forms. We can be the scribe for our kids' questions. Alternatively, we can choose to give our children strips of paper or index cards on which to write their questions down, or have table volunteers write the questions down. We need to be prepared for this process to last one to three days. Each day we do a small formative assessment on their understanding. This is where we choose any of the possible formatives assessments listed in Table 5.1 above. In this first stage, we want to assess whether or not our learners can articulate their role, the purpose of the challenge, and the final requirements or products as they are connected to the project.

If we do this during Language Arts or literacy centers, we might take anywhere from 15 to 40 minutes of each day to spend on this part. We leave ourselves additional time to devote to a word study, guided reading, big book study or other Language Arts specifics on which we are focused. If we use our entire science block for the project then we might be able to finish this in one or two days. It also depends on the ages and abilities of our kids. For additional guidance, refer back to Chapter 3 where we talked more specifically about our routines and schedules.

Visualization is key to our learners' ability to identify potential inquiry paths, as they begin their search for Finding a Solution. We want to employ an assessment method that works for us, but also ensures they see the process of discovery come alive. This is especially important in the Pre-K setting, as we strongly discourage the use of worksheets. It is important for us to think about how to draw, act, and make room for dialogue for our earliest learners so that they demonstrate their thinking. Let's think about how this visualized questioning process might specifically look in your classroom. While you may opt for one of our suggestions in Table 5.1 above, the following formalized process is one we have found to be very effective:

1   Introduce the authentic challenge and ask our learners to brainstorm possible questions and/or solutions they have.
2   Guide and support our kids to categorize the various ideas they have shared. On small strips of paper or notecards have them write what they think the solutions are to the challenge. They will also need to write what they already know about the challenge and what they want to learn in order to solve the challenge. (Preschoolers can draw or write to demonstrate their thinking to the class. Their writing will be developmentally appropriate for their age.)
3   Hang several small buckets, which can be purchased at any local discount store, in the front of the classroom. They then become an easily accessible compilation of research topics. This helps our children to get started on their research in a learner-centered way, rather than through teacher-led direction.
4   Structure a cooperative activity in which our learners share their questions before they deposit them in the buckets.

This introduction to the authentic learning experience is the first formative assessment point of our learners. In fact, we also treat it as a non-traditional pre-assessment. The inquiry questions posed by our learners help to dictate any lessons we may need to complete with some, or all, of them to backfill any gaps that may exist. These questions also confirm our ideas for scaffolding the content and skills during the entirety of the project. For some learners, we may find they need to be challenged at a higher level of thinking and we can plan appropriately to enrich the complexity of the project. Based on the knowledge that all of our learners may be at different points of entry in Bloom's, think about the value of having each learner first complete this initial questioning process on their own. Table 5.2 provides a list of scaffolded Bloom's questions to guide your assessment of our learners through this. Thus, we pre-assess to meet the needs of each child, rather than to address the needs of the class, as a whole.

As the project moves along, we don't want to forget about the questions our children have generated. As inquiry continues, our learners stumble upon new questions. These new questions continue to guide us in our support of their progress. Similarly, the initial questions serve as a guide for our kids to chart their own course in their learning, as they move toward Finding a Solution. We also suggest a periodic return to the bucket questions to formatively check for understanding. Thus, while this stage of formative assessment is the first in the project process, it is important to remember that it is also an ongoing stage.

TABLE 5.2 Entry Assessment Points through Bloom's

Bloom's Taxonomy	Question
Creating	How do we create a survival kit campaign for our parents and caregivers?
Evaluating	How does my survival kit and evacuation plan meet the physical and emotional needs of my family members and my pets?
Analyzing	How will my design ideas change for various times of the year and different weather conditions?
Applying	Based on my inferences, am I choosing the correct materials and supplies for my survival kit?
Understanding	Have I selected the right information to begin the design of my first survival kit prototype?
Remembering	What important information do I need to know before I begin to work on my challenge?

Throughout the rest of the chapter, you will see several sample sections that provide you with a generic sample of the day-to-day planning for an authentic project-based learning experience. Table 5.3 is the first in a series of five tables. For your reference and convenience, we break down the days by the Five Stages of Finding a Solution. Please note, these activities can take place during various parts of your daily schedule and are dependent on your own classroom needs and preferences. The days have two, three, or four activities listed. You may decide to increase or decrease this number. We suggest you collect the bold items for individual formative assessments. Informally, other items are formatively assessed, but not necessarily collected. Make modifications, as needed, for Pre-K and kindergarten with guided completion. This might include the need for you to record information for your learners, collaboratively complete some of the work, or ask your children to draw and explain to you these drawings.

You will also notice that some of the days are repeated in the tables. Again, this is for your convenient reference. You may find that you need to spend additional days on a particular stage or, depending on the project, you may decide to decrease the number of allotted days. These authentic challenge assessments are what are layered into and mesh with your reading and writing assessments.

TABLE 5.3 Sample of Day-to-Day Planning Guide

Day 1 – Stage 1	Day 2 – Stage 1	Day 3 – Stage 2 Information	Day 4 – Stage 2 Information	Day 5 – Stage 2 Information
Introduce the challenge	Review the challenge	Morning Meeting review of teams and **team contracts**	**Postcard prompt drawing or sentence on final product**	Literacy Stations continued
Complete a single bubble map of questions	**Learners complete a KWL with table partners**	Information gathering begins with a **Scan for Vocabulary tool**	Literacy Stations: **Interactive Journal and Scan for Vocabulary tool**	Cognitive Content Dictionary (GLAD)
Class Discussion and Concept Map creation	Concept Map bucket activity	Literacy Stations during Reader's Workshop: **Interactive Journal to capture their data and information**	Visualization activity: Be the Illustrator	**Interactive Journal rubric check** **Exit Ticket: SPACE METHOD**

Exit Ticket: reflection on their role within the project	Exit Ticket: "I am starting to think …"	Exit Ticket: Circle, Square, Triangle Reflection	Vocabulary Word Quiz	

Stage 2: Information and Prototyping

How do we know if our kids have created a viable product?

Once we know our learners have a firm grasp on the purpose of the project, it is time to transition into Stage 2. Here is where our learners gather information from multiple sources, as they deepen their search for finding the answers to their questions about the challenge. All group members gather needed information and everyone is required to be a part of this process to help design the first prototype. This first prototype becomes a physical combination of the group's ideas to address their challenge. This first draft is where and when we want their natural curiosity and creativity to shine. As educators, we don't need to redirect this creativity even if we know their ideas are not feasible. In the first draft we want our kids to begin with their own ideas, go through an iteration and feedback process, and troubleshoot or debug their designs. They will refine and change them, but the original design is still theirs. This process is a long one. It may take one to three weeks to complete it, as learners vacillate between ideas and information. Thus, it is important to continually support them based on our formative assessments.

The schedule of your project work time during any given day impacts how you move through Stage 2. There is no exact time to place this in your daily agenda, but rather the best format emerges when you connect to the literacy you embed in your project. We suggest the use of learning stations for prototyping, as listed in Table 5.4. To set up these literacy-based learning stations in our classrooms, we want to pull as many books as possible related to the challenge and the questions posed in Stage 1. These books include both fiction and nonfiction texts. During these learning stations, our learners apply

TABLE 5.4 Learning Stations for Information and Prototyping

Example Standards	Learning Stations*
RI.K.2 With prompting and support, identify the main topic and retell key details of a text	Teacher-led read-aloud of a nonfiction text
W.K.8 With guidance and support from adults, recall information from experiences or gather information from provided sources to answer a question	Inference picture cards with multiple images related to the project
RI.K.9 With prompting and support, identify basic similarities in and differences between two texts on the same topic	Multiple texts at varying levels to gather data, new vocabulary words, and identify various graphics related to the challenge
RL.K.9 With prompting and support, compare and contrast the adventure and experiences of characters in familiar stories	Fiction reading based on plot, character, and setting

*Adjustments to the learning stations need to be made in the Pre-K setting. While some children are reading at this juncture, we know most are not. Feel free to change as needed through the use of pictures, drawings, and teacher-led interactive or shared readings.

the literacy skills required in the standards. At the same time, they research and gather information for their challenge, as they move forward in finding the answers to their questions. This research is then used to help them create the first draft of their proposed solution. These learning stations encourage our learners to practice all of these literacy-based skills without even realizing it. These skills include the ability to make inferences and draw conclusions, ask and answer questions, and read for a purpose to support the information and prototyping stage. Afterwards, our learners individually document their research in concept maps and interactive journals, and scan for vocabulary worksheets. When we incorporate this individual research we have the opportunity to formatively assess reading, inference, research, and writing skills.

As our learners gather their data, we want to assess the accuracy and relevancy of the data collected to support them in Finding a Solution. This data collection occurs in many forms during this stage. While we have focused on the components of Language Arts, math is also completely embedded in this data collection process. In our weather unit, on a daily basis, during math, our kids charted the daily temperature, observed the daily weather, and reviewed the extended weather forecasts. To obtain an accurate measure of their data collection process, we graded it individually, by doing peer "I Know/You Know" information-sharing sessions and more formal quizzes. At this point in the stage, our learners are ready to create their first sample of their final solution. We want to reiterate that it is really hard to not tell them their prototypes are wrong or way out in left field, but it is important to not dash their hopes as they work toward Finding a Solution.

The information and prototyping stage of Finding a Solution provides our learners with the space to tinker, but to do so in a way that leads to the first prototype for their challenge. We typically oppose any sort of prototype model created by us. If we are the ones who cut out all the shapes, glue objects down for them, and tell them where to place their items, we reduce the level of authentic ownership for our children. Crafts may have a place within the classroom at various points in the year, but not as a part of the authentic challenge. For example, if we read multiple stories about boats, talk about boats, and allow our kids to play with toy boats, they will draw the icon they see from this interaction. When we provide models they are similar to a worksheet. Our learners will copy the model or color in the model. This type of recreation does not lead to synthesis of patterns, connections, and information. Instead, we want to promote divergent thought. As such, we first ask our learners to draw the icon of an improved boat that they visualize in their mind. From this, we see a world of difference.

Rather than merely building something for the sake of building it, our learners now chart their own conclusions in a visual way. As a teacher, the first prototype helps us to formatively assess whether or not our learners have applied accurate and relevant data to their designs. The changes from the first iteration of the prototype to the last offer us a window into the thinking of our learners, as they seek out answers in their quest to find a solution to the challenge. These windows are the perfect opportunity to conduct multiple formative assessments.

Merely looking at the prototype provides us with surface level formative assessment data. To go deeper, we must focus on a way to draw out the data from our learners. Written reflections with guiding questions probe into the thought processes that took place throughout the development of the prototype. Depending on the learner, however, these formative assessments may also be surface level; this is especially true during the first project or two. We like to take the opportunity to have one-on-one conversations with each of our learners. This creates a space for us to ask follow-up questions and causes our learners to reflect in a more targeted way. It also has the potential to provide us with better formative assessment data compared to written reflections, as some of our learners may have a difficult time expanding on their written work. Thus, while we want to continue to support and scaffold in our writing lessons, the potential difference that a personal conference may have is enlightening. This conversation is often a game changer in how we approach our lessons, scaffolding, and differentiation for our children.

We know the tinkering and maker movements have received a great deal of attention in the last few years and a hands-on approach to learning has permeated the culture of many grade levels and in many different content areas. There is, however, a fundamental difference between authentic learning experiences and establishing a makerspace or tinkerlab. Making and tinkering can support the work that we do in an authentic space. Authentic projects make room for this type of creativity in the information and prototyping stage. Table 5.5 provides you with a snapshot of what days 3 through 7 might look like in your classroom as you plan your day-to-day activities.

TABLE 5.5 Sample of Day-to-Day Planning for Second Grade

Day 3 – Stage 2 Information	Day 4 – Stage 2 Information	Day 5 – Stage 2 Information	Day 6 – Stage 2 Prototyping	Day 7 – Stage 2 Prototyping Review
Morning Meeting review of teams and **team contracts** Information gathering begins with a **Scan for Vocabulary tool** Literacy Stations during Reader's Workshop: **Interactive Journal to capture their data and information** **Exit Ticket: Circle, Square, Triangle Reflection**	**Postcard prompt drawing or sentence on final product** Literacy Stations: **Interactive Journal and Scan for Vocabulary tool** Visualization activity: Be the Illustrator **Vocabulary Word Quiz**	Literacy Stations continued Cognitive Content Dictionary (GLAD) **Interactive Journal rubric check** **Exit Ticket: SPACE METHOD**	Teamwork: 2-D prototype designs **Individual Storyboard or drawings** Up-Side Down Gallery Walk **Team Rubric Check**	Observation Charts **Team Action Plan** Expert Groups or Process Grid Investigative Reading Activities

Stage 3: Perspective and Point of View

> How do we know if our kids have thought about different ideas?

School has traditionally been about knowing the right answer or the design of a presentation that looked like it was crafted by a professional, rather than a focus on a learner's ability to find potential solutions to given challenges. This is true, even in the earliest grades. The ability to make the right phonetic sounds, count to 100, the identification of colors, and the recognition of shapes on demand are definitely foundational and necessary knowledge. However, once our learners gain ground in their understanding of this foundational knowledge, we want to push them to the level of mastery of that knowledge as they exhibit the ability to think critically about it. We also want to move our kids into a space where they consider the ideas of others. Here, the shift from breadth to depth begins, as we facilitate our learners to make connections to vocabulary words and link prior knowledge to new experiences. In any content area and at any grade level, a focus on the empowerment of our kids to think about different perspectives and points of view is paramount. Any opportunity to think about opposing views and differing ideas is a welcome space to encourage our learners to flourish in divergent thought—the ability to think creatively about many possible solutions. Table 5.6 walks you through a sample of days 8 through 12 of your planning and how each day incorporates a variety of activities to support your learners as they explore different points of view.

It is important to provide opportunities for our learners to engage and interact with experts. As we previously noted, while we may be the experts in the classroom, we aren't necessarily the experts from other career fields. Experts from other walks of life bring a fresh perspective to the work that our learners do to achieve solutions to the authentic challenge. They ask key questions that we may not think to ask. They provide valuable feedback that creates a capacity to question oneself as a learner and problem-solver.

The expert brings a wealth of information and questions that prompt the need for the second iteration of the prototype. Thus, this is a good time to bring in the expert to provide our kids feedback on their prototype. The valuable information they provide sparks improvements to the prototype. In our kindergarten weather project example,

TABLE 5.6 Sample of Day-to-Day Planning for Second Grade

Day 8 – Stage 3 Perspective and Point of View	Day 9 – Stage 3 Perspective and Point of View	Day 10 – Stage 3 Perspective and Point of View	Day 11 – Stage 3 Perspective and Point of View	Day 12 – Stage 3 Perspective and Point of View
Team Collaboration Rubric check-in Research the expert's career to help generate questions about their projects for the Ask-an-Expert session New Ideas reflection	Experts in the House: Was I an active listener? pictorial rubric **Roving Reporter writing assessment** Author Study: use a book related to the project content Prototype Trouble shooting	Prototype Trouble shooting **Sentence structure activity using project vocabulary** Mentor Text and Author Study continued	Prototype redesign: **create drawings with descriptions to highlight and clarify new or changed ideas, thoughts, and feelings** Author Study continued **Vocabulary comparison quiz**	Partner Investigative Reading Activities Team and Individual Collaboration Check-in Centers: authentic audience scenarios/role plays

our learners spent a week gathering information and a few days during their Language Arts time creating a list of the items needed for their survival kits. We brought in the State Guard to give our learners feedback on their lists and to share how they prepare for emergencies. Our children shared their lists, which included chicken nuggets, pets, pillows, stuffed animals, orange juice, coloring books, eggs, and other perishable items. Our expert listened to the children and then opened up his backpack to share its contents. He showed them that batteries need to be kept outside of the flashlight and that perishable food goes bad. He reinforced their ideas, however, with an allowance for small stuffed animals and coloring books, as they were small items. The expert session ended by having our kindergarteners go back to their lists to see if they wanted to make any changes to their survival kit. This part of the visit embedded our writing standards in the work that was completed, as our kids wrote about their reflections based on the feedback provided.

Through reflections about expert feedback, we are able to chart the changes made to the prototypes and determine whether or not the feedback was incorporated in the new iteration. Notations about how thinking was shifted, initial theories were reinforced, or ideas were completely scrapped are all things that are included in the interactive journal. Younger learners draw this process or supplement their writing with partial drawings. For some learners, the use of a flow map to diagram their changes in thinking is a valuable insight into the revision process. No matter which formative assessment tool we choose, it is important to ensure that the expert feedback does not merely fall on deaf ears, but is instead a push toward finding a more feasible final solution.

As valuable as experts are in the project, it is impossible to rely solely on their feedback to impart multiple perspectives. Building in deliberate time to require our learners to reflect on their own ideas is just as important as including expert feedback. Pose key questions and prompts for individual contemplation during strategic reflection times (Figure 5.2). These not only permit us to formatively assess learner thought processes, but also encourage individuals to articulate personal reflections regarding their current state of finding of a solution.

If we develop the time and space to listen to and evaluate the opinions of classmates, we also open up our learners to understanding the thought processes of their peers. We suggest using these prompts to initiate a conversation through guided reciprocal peer questioning. The chance to give and receive feedback, both to and from peers, is a fresh outlook for learners to consider. Fortunately, the natural curiosity of our young learners isn't clouded by years of adult perspective. This means they often encourage out of the box thinking in one another that adults sometimes dismiss.

Peer opinions, expressed through the use of role play, provide us with the opportunity to really evaluate how much consideration our kids give to one another. Role play and dramatic play is an escape from being one's self, but is also often an outlet for children to convey their true feelings. What is acted out in a role-play situation may actually be more accurate than a simple conversation between two peers. Sometimes we

Figure 5.2 Possible Prototype Reflection Prompts

- How did I arrive at my solution?
- What were other solutions I thought about using?
- What are the good things about my solution?
- What are some things to improve about my solution?
- How has my solution been influenced by the ideas of my classmates?
- How has my solution been influenced by the ideas of the expert?

provide our learners with role-play scenarios to facilitate their thinking about different perspectives. This also models the role-playing process for them to generate deeper reflection.

As our learners record the changes in their perspective throughout each stage of the challenge, we have a wealth of data to develop responses to our learners' needs. This means we can use each formative assessment point to garner our next steps for whole class instruction, mini-lessons, or individual support. Therefore, continual formative assessment is only as good as our use of it to inform our own instruction. An extensive record of our learners' thoughts and the artifacts that capture their thinking is also reflective of their growth. It illustrates the complexity of the challenge and possible solutions they continually improve upon.

This stage is important for our learners to assess their own work to make sure it is aligned with the challenge. Through Stages 1 and 2, our learners have begun to identify their personal views and use those to gather information and draw initial conclusions. This leads to the design of their first prototype. During Stage 3, it is important to look at what our learners currently view as the solution to the challenge. Next, we create opportunities for our learners to think about solutions from alternative points of view. Our goal is to assess our learners' abilities to identify the main purpose in a project and explicitly explain and describe their answer to the challenge, while simultaneously meeting the needs of their audience.

To teach our children how to understand the needs of an audience, we turn to literature and informational texts to support our lesson development. Here, we continuously ask our learners to understand a writer's purpose. We ask them to look past the text and think about the writer's intent and intended audience. Once our learners, as readers, think about the writer's point of view, they connect their thinking to the text's message or claim established by the author. When they master this skill they are able to see beyond the most basic answer: the one that is often initially reflected in their own perspective and point of view. At this stage, deciding on the purpose of their solutions for their intended audience is necessary for the improvement of their prototypes. Is the solution meant to advise, convince, or entertain? How will our learners directly meet the needs of their audience? When we have our learners analyze the author's purpose in texts, we set the stage to assess their ability to be able to do this with their own work. Our learners, in Stage 3, understand how to apply purpose and point of view to their own work, as they find solutions to the challenge.

Stage 4: Actions and Consequences

> How do we know if our kids have compared and contrasted different consequences?

We have a wonderful opportunity to weave playtime and accountability together during this stage. As prototypes are created and multiple perspectives are considered, ultimately, our kids must show documentation of the different ideas they have tested, troubleshooted, and what they enjoyed about the process. Designated and built-in reflection times compel our learners to write and share their thought processes. This is where our learners practice metacognition. Stage 4 is the time to test their actions, their beliefs about what will happen based on their solutions. Our role as teachers is to help our learners become high quality critical thinkers. In Stage 4 we foster the notion that the best thinkers think through their actions one additional time before finalizing their solutions. This is the stage that many educators skip because they run out of time, believe that young children cannot reason through the idea of consequences, or that only an adult can put the actual solution into action. Therefore, it is important to require our learners to consider their actions and the consequences of their solutions.

This stage of Finding a Solution emancipates our learners and empowers them to demonstrate their understanding of what they have learned thus far. We begin to see our learners use the academic language for the project with more confidence, as they write it in a coherent and cohesive way. We know each stage is an opportunity to assess our learners' critical thinking as they progress toward finding their own solutions and answers. However, in this stage, we specifically assess their thinking and observe their developing conclusions and evaluations as they consider the consequences of their actions. Here, we help them, through reflection, to see how their own thinking and beliefs have changed over time. Figure 5.3 provides you with question frames for your learners to determine the consequences of their actions.

To draw, write, build, and construct creates a feeling of empowerment for our children as they integrate the concepts that are contextualized in their work. These representations make up the data needed for our learners to demonstrate what they know and what they can do with the given challenge. Activities are repeated to show growth in knowledge and

Figure 5.3 Actions and Consequence Resources

Questions for Reflection
If I do X, then what things might happen? If I do not do X, then what might happen? If I do X, then what happens to Y? What if X or Y? What about X or Y?

skills as the project progresses. Check out Table 5.7 for our sample activities in days 13 to 17 that support our learners as they show us they have thought through the consequences that their actions will have on their project. For example, through the use of an interactive journal, our learners document their process and identify possible changes or modifications needed as they acquire more information and a greater understanding of the information. This journal is useful as a continual reference guide to remember important information, changes made to prototypes, and the consequences of actions taken. It demonstrates how a learner moves from a concrete, hands-on application to a 2-D pictorial prototype. In an abstract way, they present their findings. The interactive journal is similar to a concrete representation of the abstract method we use when we teach a child how to add and subtract in the early elementary grades.

This interactive progression links to the actions taken by our learners as they try possible solutions. This guides them to both visualize and

TABLE 5.7 Sample of Day-to-Day Planning for Second Grade

Day 13 – Stage 4 Actions and Consequences	Day 14 – Stage 4 Actions and Consequences	Day 15 – Stage 4 Actions and Consequences	Day 16 – Stage 4 Actions and Consequences	Day 17 – Stage 4 Actions and Consequences
SCAMPER Listen/Read/ Discuss Project text Rubric Check Writer's Workshop: **Individual writing piece: "How to Book"**	SCAMPER Team Project storywheel: visualize and summarize the story of how teams worked together **Reflection: My team helps me to do ____ better**	Share and Share Alike: Product changes and presentation practice Presentation rubric reflection **Team Check- in: "How am I doing?"**	Think Aloud Role Play Continued project work time **Exit Ticket: If my product does ____ what will happen to ____?**	Work time to improve or make changes based on feedback Teamwork rubric check **Exit Ticket: I used to think/ Now I think**

rationalize the consequences that result from those actions. In short, they look at the impact their possible solutions will have on people, places, and things to decide what will be good and what will be bad. They have to decide which solution provides them with the most return on their action, while limiting the potential negative impacts it may require.

At this point, we need to determine what tools we will embed in our daily schedule to encourage our learners to fully discuss their ideas. This gives them not only the tools, but the time to justify and make any desired changes. This justification is what is often left out of the equation when learners solve problems, as the process requires a deep level of critical thinking. Rather than simply proposing a solution, our children now have to explain their choices, the impact of those choices, and why the good may outweigh the bad. This stage is where natural curiosity turns into true creativity.

There are many tools we can use to support this process while formatively assessing our learners' abilities to think about what they know, to make connections, and visualize outcomes. For instance, let's review our SCAMPER assessment, from Mind Tools. This is the brainstorming technique we first discussed in Chapter 4 that encourages the improvement of existing ideas. Remember that SCAMPER is a mnemonic that stands for substitute, combine, adapt, modify, put to another use, eliminate, and reverse. We know this vocabulary isn't necessarily developmentally appropriate for young learners. It is up to us to modify and make it accessible for our early learners. For example, instead of substitute, we might use the word "change." Instead of combine, we use the words "put together." For instance, in our weather unit, after the visit from our State Guardsman, we asked our kids what changes they needed to make to their kits. We then compared urgent weather situations to other emergencies that might occur. Our class created anchor charts for these other crisis type situations that showed how they could adapt their kits for other emergency events. From their engagement in the SCAMPER method, our kids came up with the idea to add an emergency contact list. The emergency contacts they chose included not only their parents, but also other possible contacts in case their parents could not be reached.

At this point, you might be wondering how to use this same tool in the Pre-K classroom. We like the use of SCAMPER and find it to be successful as we challenge our littlest kiddos to redefine their dramatic play center. As they make the choices for changes, they take greater pride and ownership in the centers. In short, no matter what grade level you teach, we encourage you to try this tool and the many others we have listed in Table 5.1.

Stage 5: Considerations and Conclusions

> How do we know if our kids have reached the best possible solution
> for their audience?

Just like good readers identify the cause and effect in a story, good
problem-solvers look for the consequences of their actions. Once our
learners have thought about the consequences, it is time to transition
their thinking to summarize their considerations and draw their final
conclusions. While it is easy for a child to jump to conclusions without putting much thought into the reasons for those conclusions, it is
our responsibility to mentor them through this and the previous four
stages of Finding a Solution. The four stages inform our planning for
appropriate supports, as needed. However, Stage 5 cannot overlook
the importance of the need to continue that support and prepare for
their presentations or exhibitions. If we have continually implemented
formative assessments, by the time we reach the considerations and
conclusions stage, the outcome of the summative assessment should
not be a surprise. The summative assessment now becomes a celebra-
tion of the learning that has taken place.

At this stage, we move into the final stretch of the project with our
learners. So far, they have worked hard to demonstrate what they know,
had many successes with their process of troubleshooting and debug-
ging their prototypes, and reflected continuously. At this juncture, our
kids represent the potential solutions to the challenge that they tried
and, at some point, rejected. Through this representation, clear indica-
tions surface as to why some of the possible solutions would not work
versus why they chose the solution on which they finally settled. It is
also another point in the process to transfer their prediction and inference skills they have employed throughout the project. Table 5.8 details
a sample of your final days of the project. You will notice that this is
the stage that lends itself to story writing. It uses the beginning, middle,
and end strategy for younger children and the writing process for older
kids. These are the strategies we already use to teach writing throughout the year. Now their project work can be expressed in the form of a
narrative or expository piece. For example, a "How to Book" is a great
individual summative assessment that not only uses our writing standards, but guides our children to reflect on their learning and choices
made throughout the project.

TABLE 5.8 Sample of Day-to-Day Planning for Second Grade

Day 17 – Stage 4 Actions and Consequences	Day 18 – Stage 5 Considerations and Conclusions	Day 19 – Stage 5 Considerations and Conclusions	Day 20 – Stage 5 Considerations and Conclusions	Day 21 – Stage 5 Considerations and Conclusions
Work time to improve or make changes based on feedback Teamwork rubric check **Exit Ticket: I used to think/ Now I think**	Final Independent Draft SWOT analysis (Good, Grow, Possible, Buggy) **Personal presentation reflection: my own check-in**	Audience Role Play: how to be a respectful, fair, and attentive audience member Video pair presentations reflections	Frame-by-Frame Approach Writer's Workshop to complete final written piece	Celebrations and reflections

TABLE 5.9 The Frame-by-Frame Approach

Decision Frame 1	Decision Frame 2	Decision Frame 3	Decision Frame 4
• My first idea	• What was good about my idea	• What I didn't like about my idea	• What I changed about my idea
• My second idea	• What was good about my idea	• What I didn't like about my idea	• What I changed about my idea
• My third idea	• What was good about my idea	• What I didn't like about my idea	• What I changed about my idea

The age and grade level of the child determines the amount of detail related to the descriptions of rejected solutions. It also depends on when and where in our daily schedule we choose to do this stage. We see successful project-based learning teachers utilize their writer's workshop time for this because of the quality and amount of writing teachers expect to see. At the same time, the presentations for a public audience can be worked on in short spurts during reader's workshop or science/ social studies time. Younger children may illustrate their choices and use simplified sentences. We suggest having the illustrations follow a frame-by-frame approach, as noted in Table 5.9, to visually represent the decision-making process. These four frames guide the thinking process, but feel free to include additional frames if a learner needs to tell more of the story. We use this model for as many ideas as our individuals or groups of learners have proposed. We recommend the requirement of at least three different ideas or modifications to at least three ideas.

We sometimes, however, find as many as five or six proposed and modified or rejected ideas. While we have introduced you to the frame-by-frame approach in Stage 5, it may also be appropriate to incorporate it in an earlier stage, as determined by our learners' progress and needs for support.

When our kids work in groups, we have them complete the frame-by-frame approach on an individual basis before adding to the group's collective document. This provides us with a detailed individual assessment, rather than a guess of who may be leading a group think. Older children may not need to draw their ideas. However, we encourage drawing as a differentiation tool for those that need it. In either case, a focus on the inclusion of key vocabulary terms, reasoning strategies, and justifications of their final decisions is imperative.

Throughout the project process, it is just as important for our young learners to articulate why they rejected solutions as it is for them to justify why they accepted others. They master content standards as they troubleshoot and debug their prototypes. When they talk about how they drew conclusions and decided what solutions and ideas weren't suited for their final answer we move into the evaluation and creativity levels of Bloom's Taxonomy. Part of the ability to think critically comes through in their explanations of why something does not work or, in some cases, why a solution isn't suited for their authentic audience. This is where we should see kids focus on a variety of questions. What does my audience need? Is this what they want? Will they like my drawings? Will they understand what I am talking about? These considerations also take into account the relevancy of the conclusions. For example, our learners needed to develop a weather emergency kit suitable for their families who live in a tornado prone area, but generally don't have access to a basement. If our children were preparing a weather emergency kit and evacuation plan and lived on the coast of California, they would have had to take into account the potential for an earthquake rather than a tornado.

As our learners push toward the final days of their authentic learning experience, we can't forget to continue to formatively assess the work they complete. It is easy, at the end of a project, to focus on the scheduled presentation or putting the final touches on a piece to be showcased. However, these last days can be the most critical in terms of assessment. Did our learners answer all of their original inquiry questions? Have they arrived at an acceptable conclusion after making multiple considerations? Can they clearly articulate why they believe their conclusion to be the best solution for the given challenge? If we have done enough formative assessment throughout the project process, the answers to these questions should not surprise us. However, we want to ensure that things don't fall apart in the last few days of the challenge. This is a great place for us to implement our version of the SWOT protocol (Good, Grow, Possible, Buggy) for our learners to review all of their work. What are the strengths, weaknesses, opportunities, and threats their final solution might face when reviewed by experts? Of course, for our younger kids, we will once again want to modify our language. Instead, when needed, shift to the use of what is good, how their solution gets better through growth, what new things are possible, or what is buggy about the final solution. Another great tool for this stage is the spider web discussion. We have our learners freely discuss the challenge without us interrupting them. This will provides us with a lens into their thinking and reflection on learning. Just remember that the younger the children, the smaller the groups need to be for the discussion. We have successfully implemented a spider web discussion with preschoolers, but don't put more than four in a conversation. By the time our children reach third grade, they are ready for eight to ten in a group.

Ultimately, we have to come to the end of a project experience. We know that in the world outside of the classroom, authentic learning experiences continue to present challenges for those that try to solve them. Think about your latest cell phone. How different is it from the first one you owned? How frequently do you purchase a new one in order to get the latest and greatest features? The same holds true in any project-based learning experience our kids tackle. While the challenge may never be truly over in an authentic sense, we have time constraints that require us to limit the amount of time we allow the challenge to extend. The good news is we can repeat the same project in a subsequent year. We just have to make a few tweaks and adjustments to account for the work that was completed in the prior year or to reflect our current classroom of learners.

Through the completion of multiple formative assessment strategies in each of the Five Stages of Finding a Solution, our learners have effectively produced a portfolio of their growth and mastery of the content and standards. Each formative assessment opportunity is also one for us to adjust our support and instruction to meet the needs of all our learners. From the first formative assessment in Stage 1, which includes the bucket list of questions, to the final use of the frame-by-frame approach in Stage 5, growth happens. These formative assessments, collectively, tell a story of the learning that has occurred. By maximizing the formative assessments in our project, with Strategy Four, we have charted the inquiry process that was spurred by our kids' own natural curiosity. What are your next steps? Reflect here, before you move onto the following chapter, on how you maximize formative assessment in your project.

Where are You? **What are You Thinking?** **How do You Feel?**		
Take Action	**Seek Community**	**Think Aloud**
Choose one formative assessment tool which you have never used in your classroom. Implement the tool into your daily routine at least twice. Record the data and analyze how the tool helped your kids to demonstrate their understanding of the learning target.	Share your results with a teaching partner and solicit feedback. Be sure to discuss the impact the data had on you and how you adjusted your instruction to reflect the needs of your learners.	After reading this chapter and implementing at least one formative assessment tool, how has your instruction been affected? Reflect on how your learners responded to the tool and its impact on your instruction.

6

Strategy Five: Activate Intrinsic Motivation

How do I activate intrinsic motivation through an authentic project?

We would like you to take a moment and answer a few questions. Jot down your answers on whatever paper you have laying around. Don't stop to think about the questions for too long. Simply, write the first words and phrases that come to your mind.

- ◆ What personally motivates you?
- ◆ What motivated you when you were a kid?
- ◆ What motivated you to read this book?
- ◆ What motivates your learners in your classroom?

Chances are, if we were to have all of our readers of this book submit their answers, we would find similar, generalized responses. If we made our questions more specific we would begin to identify what motivates you in certain situations or at certain times of your life. Some of us may focus more on external rewards, such as grades, a higher pay scale, or an advanced degree. On the other hand, curiosity sparks learners to explore and be spontaneous through the intrinsic motivation they experience (Muller and Louw, 2004). These are the things that help us to solve the problems we face in life, as adults, such as improved self-esteem or a higher quality of life. These intrinsic motivators tend to be the more powerful ones and push us to make changes (Knowles, Holton, and Swanson, 2005). For our early Pre-K to third grade learners, intrinsically motivating factors may include outdoor playtime, time with others to share stories, or the experience of new challenges. These activities give them choice and autonomy while they gain advancement in the levels of their skills. They also mirror the "curiosity, exploration, spontaneity, and interest" noted by Muller and Louw. Ultimately, no matter what the activity, there is something deep inside of us that pushes us to try just a little harder, work just a little longer, and create just a little more. Whatever that something is, we classify it as what satisfies and motivates us. It is intrinsic motivation. Strategy Five, activate intrinsic motivation, promotes the social and emotional development of children who are eager and willing to learn, as they contribute to their own success. This is in lieu of a teacher who tells them they are successful.

How do I activate intrinsic motivation through an authentic project? Before we can answer this question, we need to understand the difference between intrinsic and extrinsic motivation. Let's compare our above definition of intrinsic motivation to extrinsic motivation. How many times have your kids participated in an activity simply because you told them to do so? Was it merely to please you, as their teacher? If so, it was completed due to extrinsic motivation. The reward came from the approval you provided. This reward must be continually given in order to maintain a high level of extrinsic motivation. If you have a reward jar that you fill with pompoms, chain links your kids earn, or stickers placed on a chart that your kids receive for good behavior, you can relate to the use of extrinsic motivators to persuade your learners to complete a task. When they are compliant, they get the reward. However, you have probably also experienced a gradual decrease in that behavior as they forget about the reward jar, the links, or decide they could not care less about yet another sticker.

Take Note: Motivation and rewards are not the same thing. They are, however, interwoven into our daily schedule and routines to support simple tasks and higher level thinking. Motivation is the reason we do something, while rewards are what you get for doing something. Rewards can be either intrinsic or extrinsic in nature. Extrinsic rewards are controlled by an outside force, namely, you, the teacher. Intrinsic rewards are related to the internal pride a child feels when they accomplish good work.

Extrinsic motivation is what pushes kids to focus on grades. We know, at the Pre-K to second grade levels, for some schools, number and letter grades don't always come into play. The reinforcement of this extrinsic motivation, however, sets the stage for this as an emphasis in later years. Although, if you are using a skill-based grading system, you might already see some of your higher achievers worried about receiving an advanced or proficient mark in some areas. At the third grade level, you may have experienced this with some or many of your learners. We want to reverse this thought process for kids, parents, and you, the teacher, through the implementation of authentic project-based learning experiences. A focus on grades can lead to a decrease in the natural curiosity we strive to enhance. It also has the potential to push our kids to the point of ambivalence about school if they feel they can't make the grade. However, at the same time, we know that grades are often a district necessity. Therefore, we balance this out with the use of the formative assessment tools we discussed in Chapter 5. We also call out the differences between extrinsic and intrinsic motivation in Table 6.1.

TABLE 6.1 Extrinsic versus Intrinsic Motivation

Stages of Finding a Solution	Extrinsic Motivation	Intrinsic Motivation
Stage 1: Authentic Challenge and Purpose	• An exciting launch to the project challenge • Your excitement, as the teacher, about the project	• Connection to the community • Personally relevant to the child
Stage 2: Information and Prototyping	• Possible off-site field trip • Use of lots of manipulatives	• Answers to inquiry questions • Build something from scratch
Stage 3: Perspective and Point of View	• An engaging guest speaker • Role-play activities to represent ideas	• Gain a broader sense of the world • An authentic audience for the final product
Stage 4: Actions and Consequences	• Participation in a fun experiment • Complete one activity to move on to the next	• Ability to eliminate possibilities on their own • Allowance for trial and error
Stage 5: Considerations and Conclusions	• Knowledge that the end of the project is in sight • The grade or "good job" at the end	• Proud of their own developed solution • Solution has a potential to effect change

The key to authentic project-based learning design is to understand that our learners are not unmotivated. Similarly to you and us, they are just motivated by different things. We have established by now that our children have natural curiosity. The more we develop that natural curiosity, the deeper we tap into their intrinsic motivation. If we foster the curiosity our children have, we help to increase their potential to learn new things. This builds their confidence and provides a space for them to learn and grow. Thus, it is up to us to develop or co-develop with our children an authentic learning experience that will expand their confidence as they grow and learn. This authentic learning experience also has the potential to focus on the exploration, spontaneity, and interest that are key components of intrinsic motivation.

We find that teachers, as they start to explore authentic project design, like to plan out the entire project from start to finish on exactly how their learners will develop their answer. This is because they can rely on their own resources and own experiences and will not encounter too many surprises. They feel like this is a good beginning point, as they are comfortable with it. There definitely isn't anything wrong with starting here. However, since you are reading this book, you are probably already intrinsically motivated to move beyond the past projects that you've tried. But, first, we want you to understand that not every challenge needs to be intrinsically motivating for 100 percent of your class, 100 percent of the time. We know as adults that our motivations wax and wane during a project. We know certain areas may require more work or feel harder than others. The same holds true for our children and this is something we must keep in mind as we move forward in our own journey of authentic project-based learning.

We need to carve out the space for the various things in a project that motivate kids for relevant reasons. So, how do you influence your learners' motivations? How are your kids' motivations influenced by outside factors? How can you capitalize on those outside influences to tap into their intrinsic motivation?

In an authentic challenge, we always take care to ensure the work is learner-centered and relevant, and that our kids are engaged throughout the process. We provide time for them to have autonomy in the various Stages of Finding a Solution. We also embed our learners' likes and areas of interest into our daily routine and, more specifically, their stages of learning. To a certain extent, we can control those circumstances. As the teacher, our role is to create the bridge between an authentic challenge and our curricular requirements. We must also encourage our children to share their likes, wants, and needs in class in order to ensure we provide relevant connections to the factors that influence them. Here, we want to move beyond engagement and into empowerment.

Often teachers hear the word engagement and assume the need to entertain their kids throughout the challenge. A high quality challenge is one that our kids own and we can help them own it when we connect their strengths and prior knowledge to the work. This begins to push the challenge into a space of empowerment for our learners. To start this process, try a simple Venn diagram. Place a picture of the authentic challenge from your classroom perspective in one circle and a picture of their life outside of school in the other one. As a class, look for relevant, personal connections to the challenge at school, at home, and where they have connections to both. Children love to share about themselves for both circles of the diagram. Our role is to help them see where the overlap between the two happens, as our kids learn best from their own creations. In fact, our Pre-K children are the most eager to start any task that begins with their curiosity. In any case, and at any age, our goal is to resist the urge to tell them how to create something or what it should look like at the end, as this is where the link between intrinsic motivation and the natural curiosity of our kids is forged.

Intrinsic motivation is a constantly moving target. It begins in Stage 1 of Finding a Solution and continues to play out through each stage. The strengths of our kids are brought to the surface during teamwork and with individual work. The intrinsic motivation will vacillate for each learner, so there is a need for us to constantly monitor his or her motivations throughout each stage. We want our learners to gauge their own social and emotional development and reflect on what they like doing and how they can improve. The important thing is to ensure our learners feel they have the power to potentially effect change through engaging in the authentic challenge. That change may be as uncomplicated as a butterfly contribution to the garden, the creation of a sailboat adventure on the playground, or the organization of a school store to do a bake sale fundraiser.

Motivations might change from project to project. Consider this as you design any authentic project-based learning experience and think about what you can do to maintain motivation. Part of what we must remember is that ownership in learning leads to intrinsic motivation. For example, in a given challenge, our learners design their first prototype. But, we know their learning and experiences throughout the project cause them to make improvements to the prototype. This happens at the various Stages of Finding a Solution. Subsequently, with each new prototype, they deepen their sense of ownership, which increases their feelings of accomplishment and satisfaction. Thus, we see the need to take the time to recognize the areas of our day where we provide autonomy for our young learners. This is a first step to identifying where our kids feel intrinsically motivated. When children are intrinsically motivated, they are more likely to try new things, solve problems, and attack challenges with a newfound excitement.

We know we have a different classroom of personalities every year. One year, our daily job chart motivates our class; the next year, our reader's workshop takes center stage. Accordingly, extrinsic motivation has its place in our classrooms and there is nothing wrong with having extrinsic motivation at certain points in the project. For instance, we need to engage our children in the challenge from the beginning. This means, we need to launch the challenge in such a way that it grabs the attention of our learners and gets them excited about their participation in finding a solution. However, if the challenge is intrinsically motivating for our learners, it is unlikely that the excitement about the project will wane. Thus, a personally relevant challenge that connects to the community of our learners helps to propel them forward in their desire to find a solution. This is also true for many of the activities that we complete in the classroom. A fun experiment or exciting field trips, as stand-alone activities, are great for our children. However, to maintain this level of engagement, we need to link together these types of activities and allow our kids to develop or build something on their own and for review by an authentic audience. Similarly, for our Pre-K kids, free play is an important component of their school day. As such, we need to encourage a culture of play. However, we can approach our authentic challenges at this level in a spirit of guided play, initiated by us, the teacher, but directed by our kids. Play is a critical component in early childhood growth and development. In Pre-K, our young learners thrive off the classroom culture and community. They use it to mature and transform their cognitive processes through play. The art of play allows them to use their natural curiosities and intrinsic motivations as they experience new and repeated situations. These repeated experiences and situations are the building blocks for a child's social-emotional capacity, memory, and thinking. Problem-solving is anchored in these situations and experiences. Without the repeated opportunity to play and explore, the vehicle for developing natural curiosity and intrinsic motivation, we limit their opportunities to acquire the necessary tools needed to build their social-emotional, communication, collaboration, critical thinking, and creativity skills.

If you currently rely on the extrinsic rewards we discussed at the start of this chapter in order to increase motivation in your classroom, that's okay. There is nothing to say that you can't continue to use them. Stickers, a choice gift from the prize box, or an ice cream party are rewards that motivate some children. However, extrinsic motivation, based on rewards, tends to produce less consistent effort, as there is a decreased value placed on the task at hand. Additionally, in some cases, the extrinsic motivation may be linked to the avoidance of punishment, as children believe they should act a certain way or complete a particular task. Conversely, the more authentic and the more relevant our project-based learning experience is for our kids, the more we see a favorable shift to intrinsic motivation. We design the learning experiences and we design the learning environment, and, therefore, we are in control of the level of intrinsic motivation within our classroom at any given time.

Think about the areas of your day that provide you with opportunities to stimulate your learners' intrinsic motivations. The intrinsic motivation to learn happens when activities are perceived as enjoyable and interesting to our children. The more we tap into the natural curiosity in the early grades, the less likely our children are to lose their intrinsic motivation. We make the learning a memorable experience and one that empowers our kids to potentially effect change. Our perspective of change can be as a big as a school-wide presentation or as small as a plant that produces green beans in the school's garden. In either case, we create lifelong learners who develop a sense of wonder about their world. This, then, persists into higher grade levels and at higher cognitive functions.

Situational Motivation

We've spent a good bit of time differentiating between extrinsic and intrinsic motivation and we really like how Guay, Vallerand, and Blancard (2000) take things a bit further than this. They discuss what they call a situational motivation scale. Depending on the situation, our learners may exhibit any of these types of motivation at any given time. They can also possibly shift from one situation to another during the course of a project and between any of the four types of motivation (Table 6.2). However, a properly designed authentic project-based learning experience is supposed to avoid the amotivation category. Even so, no matter how authentic and how relevant the challenge, if the

TABLE 6.2 Situational Motivation Scale

Amotivation	External Regulation	Identified Regulation	Intrinsic Motivation
"I'm not smart." "I am not a good reader."	"Tell me what I need to know. I'll remember it." "I want to make my teacher happy."	"What we are learning is okay." "This project is better than doing worksheets."	"I can't wait to work on this project!" "I have the chance to make something new and useful."

challenge is not scaffolded well, amotivation is bound to set in with some kids. A book that is too difficult to read, a math concept that hasn't been properly explained, or even a poorly worded challenge question has the potential to result in kids who become easily frustrated.

Your best students, and we refer to them as students rather than learners in this respect, are the ones who focus on external regulation. This external regulation may also include extrinsic rewards as part of their motivation. Even at this early age, you know the ones who have started to figure out what we call the game of school. These children want to please their teachers, their parents, and want to do well in school, because that is what is expected. In some cases, what is expected is tied to a reward when the expectation is met. Here, what is "learned" is often short-lived as it is based on external regulation. Unless the information is frequently used, it is pushed to the recesses of the brain and may or may not be retrieved in the future. Thus, with a design of an authentic learning experience, the goal is to diminish the external regulation. Rather than the need to please someone who has no direct tie to the outcome of the challenge, our learners focus on their authentic audience.

Those children, who aren't concerned about external forces to drive them to perform well in school are probably the ones in your classrooms who aren't necessarily excited about the work that is asked of them. They may not complain either. These kiddos don't find a particular activity boring, but they aren't enthusiastic about it. They typically go along with it to get it finished and are just glad that it isn't another worksheet to complete. You may have already tried a project with these children only to see these types of results. If this is the case, we urge you to use your newfound knowledge on authentic project design to reflect on what areas of that project need to be strengthened. Chances are your original project design lacked an open-ended challenge made relevant to the lives of your learners. We know that in the very first stage of Finding a Solution, it is critical for our learners to make meaningful connections to their own experiences. For this reason, we have to be intentional to include activities that allow our learners to visually or orally articulate their own connections. Also, the potential to effect change may have been absent from the project design. To that end, if our learners do not make personal connections it can be difficult for an individual or team to connect their solution to the authentic challenge. Although our learners do not need to have their solution aligned immediately to the challenge, they should be certain about how they personally can relate to it.

During the project-based learning experience, if we allow our learners to simmer in ambiguity, rather than provide them with the one right answer, we actually foster intrinsic motivation. The first stage is also your first opportunity for your learners to generate more questions and think about personal experiences, and for you as a teacher to ask guiding questions that help them make connections as they ponder the unknown. Sometimes, we fail to recognize that our learners really like the challenge of being given an open-ended problem that they need to solve. This stimulates the thinking and growth that our children do as learners. While trial and error is often frustrating for us as adults, the natural curiosity that is inherent in our young children lends itself to an enjoyable experience as they troubleshoot their ideas and move toward a final solution.

If we haven't already convinced you that intrinsic motivation is an important element in the development of the natural curiosity of our learners, let's take a look at what intrinsic motivation helps to minimize in the classroom. Children who have high levels of intrinsic motivation are anxious to jump into project work, rather than exhibiting high levels of anxiety about working on the project. Fewer distractions are apparent in the classroom. Learners focus on the task at hand, rather than wandering around the room, jumping from learning station to learning station, or instigating a problem with other kids. The stress that many children experience, especially in the second and third grades, with an increase in homework and responsibilities, diminishes as they engage in the authentic challenge. Instead of a concern about the completion of work, because it is required, the focus shifts to the desire to delve deeply into the work in order to find a solution. Finally, the lack of confidence that children experience at various points during a school year starts to disappear. As our learners propose solutions to an authentic audience and receive positive feedback, they flourish as confident innovators.

Intrinsic motivation, leads to a decrease in ...	Your role in supporting intrinsic motivation is to ...
◆ anxiety ◆ distractions ◆ lack of confidence ◆ stress	◆ help learners set attainable goals ◆ recognize individual contributions ◆ redirect, but don't discourage ◆ offer verbal and nonverbal encouragement

Through our own work with authentic learning experiences, we have seen a marked increase in the persistence our learners display at any given task. Our learners troubleshoot their prototypes, receive feedback from experts and peers, and work toward finding a solution with a vigor that strengthens the natural curiosity they inherently possess. This leads to less surface-level learning and instead, increased academic performance is traced to greater retention of content and the honing of skills. These, collectively, increase the intrinsic motivation that occurs in our learners.

A well-designed, authentic project-based learning experience automatically increases the level of intrinsic motivation of your learners. However, there are a few things we can do in order to maintain it throughout the project. It is important to give as much meaningful verbal and nonverbal encouragement to our learners, as possible. This doesn't mean we have to resort to the extrinsic rewards of sticker charts or smiley faces. However, just as we like to receive targeted affirmation for a job well done, so do our children. We want to be careful not to discourage our kids. Sometimes, we might notice a child that is straying from the topic at hand. Here, we want to acknowledge their interest, but, in a caring way, remind them they need to get back on track or ask them to explain how their work connects to the task at hand and provide its purpose. Additionally, we want to recognize individual contributions to the group's work. Often, if we don't keep a careful watch on teamwork, one or more kids may feel left out. Worse yet, a child may try to take credit for work he or she hasn't done. Finally, we can work with our learners to set attainable goals. While some children are inclined to set their own goals, most, at this age, are not. We facilitate this process and help our learners in their articulation of how they intend to attain their goals. We ask what we can do to support them in this quest, as this is equally important. Also, regular checks on how well they are meeting these goals should not be ignored. It is a great way to help personalize the learning of our children. In short, no matter how great the challenge is from the outset of the project launch, a failure to do many of these things will ultimately see the level of intrinsic motivation wane.

For those of us teaching Pre-K and kindergarten, our goal is to start our youngest learners on the road to becoming independent learners. Intrinsic motivation starts with them being able to actively seek help from themselves and their peers. This includes modeling processes such as "see three before me." The more independent they become as learners, the more intrinsically motivated they are by the process.

Collaborative Teamwork

We view teamwork as a compound word representative of how two pieces come together to form one entity that works toward a common goal. Group work, on the other hand, is a separate set of entities that work on something together, but have different goals. Through our work, we have discovered that when the work is authentic, our teams of learners come together because they are intrinsically motivated to find a collaborative solution. In the classroom, our role is to utilize the highs and lows of communication and collaboration to demonstrate for our learners the strengths in collaborative teamwork. Collaborative teamwork is developmentally appropriate for children at this age, because it is a critical time for our young children to experience the process of forming a team. They come together for a purpose, engage in conflict, find ways to cooperate, move toward collaboration, and find closure through the culmination of their experience. As members of a team, our children learn to mitigate their emotions and develop their communication skills. Teamwork enhances the intrinsic motivation our kids experience during a project-based challenge.

We know children naturally form teams through play and exploration. This means we foster their natural curiosity about other children and things when they are engaged in meaningful experiences. Young children learn with others, yet they need to also construct the learning for themselves. Authentic challenges provide the space where collaborative curiosity takes place and all our learners have the opportunity to influence the possible solution at various times and in different directions.

Traditional cooperative learning strategies are the tools you use to build the communication skills of your learners when they are in newly formed teams. These might include methods such as shoulder partners, carousel feedback, round robin, or round table. These are the tools that are probably already familiar to your kids. We want you to continue to use what works for you. However, think about the ways in which these tools are most effectively integrated into your daily routines in order to activate your learners' intrinsic motivation. Rather than presenting a seemingly unrelated series of activities that require our children to work in teams and, in some cases, dread that teamwork, focus on how the collaboration helps them to solve the challenge. Support from others, coupled with our facilitation of the process, feeds their confidence as learners and their ability to find a solution to the challenge.

Our intent, at this developmental stage in our learners' lives, is to build their independence and confidence. Our daily schedules and routines shed light on the windows of opportunity for our learners to practice their independence skills. We layer these skills, over time, to gradually release the responsibility of the learning to them. This learning takes shape with centers, job roles, and, in Pre-K, unstructured and structured play. As each year passes, we increase their level of independence and responsibility, as our children mature socially and behaviorally. Thus, we see an improvement from year to year in their proficiency as team members.

There are many ways to build the collaboration and communication skills necessary for our learners to function well as team members. Parachute play leads to a discussion about how teams work together. The use of a T-chart is great to model a list of good and growing team behaviors. Older kids can co-develop a teamwork rubric, while younger learners engage in a discussion about examples that would fit within the given rubric. Additionally, a shared writing or drawing activity is a great place to practice writing while imaginatively creating a story about a fictional teammate. All of these options improve the functions of teams within your authentic project.

Children are intrinsically motivated to become a good teammate and be part of a team. Therefore, teamwork allows them to express themselves through their actions during a variety of learning experiences. Imagination, creativity, and their symbolic behaviors (reading, writing, singing, playing, dancing, researching) emerge when our learners are given extended time and space to form positive collaborative teams. Our role is to provide our young learners with these experiences so they practice the actions of teaming through their authentic project. When they truly become members of a team, they begin to satisfy their natural curiosities through collaboration and cooperation when finding a solution to any given challenge.

Here are a few points to keep in mind when your learners work in teams:

- ◆ Model effective team strategies and role-play positive interactions with others to reinforce their sense of classroom community. As we know, at this age, many children have a high need of acceptance from their peers.
- ◆ Monitor and assess collaborative groups through repeated shared and sustained dialogue. Do this in both whole and small group settings, between adults and children, and children and their teams.
- ◆ Allow for productive struggle, but use your knowledge of social and emotional development to intervene when learners are struggling too much.
- ◆ Create a space for mentors and community partners to play a role in the teaming process, as they provide support, feedback, and guiding questions.

As we move away from group work and toward a classroom community that is built on collaborative teamwork, we find it is easy to activate intrinsic motivation in our learners. It is natural for them to want to work together at various points in their learning experience. As we facilitate the process, we not only help to build their collaboration and communication skills, but we also strengthen their imaginations as their natural curiosity is piqued through the authentic challenge. This also prepares them for the social interactions that take place as they work with community partners.

Community Partnerships

We want to expose our learners to experts within the community that support their quest to find a solution to their authentic challenge. These experts help to bring their solutions and products to fruition and bridge the gap between what's pretend and what's real. In an authentic challenge, we create the context for our children to use play and creativity to design for the here and now. The real challenges we ask them to tackle are tied to their sense of reality and their local community. When a child gives back to the community, their sense of accomplishment is unparalleled. While it may seem premature to put this responsibility on our early elementary children, it is never too soon to start. In fact, if we lay the foundation now, those lessons carry over later in life. Accordingly, if we design an authentic learning experience that taps into our community resources, we model this process for them and engage them in their community.

We noted in Chapter 1 that an early learner's community is limited. Remember, we may need to start within our school community before we branch out to the greater community at large. Whatever the case, if we build these partnerships early on, we increase the scope of the community we target. We are also able to bring the community into our classrooms. Any interaction that we have with the community and experts within the community, add to our learners' feelings of pride. When we connect our young people to adults and with authentic and relevant challenges, a sense of purpose pervades everything they do. This sense of purpose provides our learners with a desire to do well and creates enjoyment in the learning process. The learning focus shifts away from "why do we need to do this?" Instead, it moves to "I can't wait to get started!"

In true authentic project-based learning experiences, we want to develop and cultivate long-term partnerships as often as possible. This is the difference between using community resources and creating community partnerships that we explore in more detail in Table 6.3. Partnerships foster long-term growth and learning compared to an annual consumable. While there is nothing wrong with taking a field trip to a local site, think about how you could take that field trip a step further to turn it into an authentic challenge. This is similar to the zoo project we discussed in Chapter 1.

As we build our community partnerships, the ideas for authentic challenges multiply. In fact, our expert network continues to grow as we create more partnerships. This network helps ensure we move beyond service learning projects and into a space where critical thinking is key in the authentic challenge design.

TABLE 6.3 Community Connections

Community Resources	Community Partnerships
Take a tour of a local manufacturing plant	Help to redesign the tour of the manufacturing plant to address kid friendly questions
Visit the local historical society	Design an exhibit for an upcoming showcase on local history that is age appropriate for elementary school visitors
Take a hike at a local state park or recreation area	Map out an exercise program for elementary kids to complete for one of the easier hiking trails
Take a walking tour of the grocery store and visit with the nutritionist on staff	Plan and prepare a well-balanced meal to be served for parents at back to school night

Critical Thinking to Intrinsically Motivate

The art of thinking is one that is molded and improved by metacognition and thinking about our thinking. Whether we realize it or not, our youngest learners are excellent critical thinkers. Their natural curiosity causes them to try, try, and try again as they learn to walk, to hold a crayon, and to build and manipulate objects. This exhibits an innate intrinsic motivation. As adults, without even realizing it, we automatically scaffold learning for our young children as they grow, to foster this intrinsic motivation. As our children enter Pre-K, we continue this support through the use of explicitly crafted questions, visual cues, and reflection. This helps our kids learn to articulate and visualize their thinking and learning processes. The use of visual cues, concept maps, and the draft and prototype processes for critical thinking are important. They build self-awareness as our kids see at what stages they are thinking critically through each Stage of Finding a Solution. This makes learning more enjoyable for them, as the level of frustration wanes and is replaced with a sense of accomplishment. The intrinsic motivation to learn happens when activities are perceived as enjoyable and interesting. To help you visualize the Stages of Finding a Solution as they relate to critical thinking, refer to Table 6.4. You may remember this as Table 2.1 from Chapter 2.

We want to design a visual space that maps the Stages of Finding a Solution as teams or individuals progress through the critical thinking process. When we think about curating our classroom community we want to create a visually supportive space to enhance critical thinking and cultivate intrinsic motivation, along with calendar charts, word walls, and birthday celebrations. Later, in Chapter 8, we address critical thinking more specifically and ways to apply it. Since we have already discussed the revised Bloom's Taxonomy in great detail, let's jump right into how we do it. We design our lessons, activities, and literacy components according to the levels of Bloom's. Our learners focus on whichever stage they are thinking through. In our classrooms, depending on the setup of the project, we either have our kids' pictures or the project team names move through each of the stages. For example, we create a poster for each stage. Underneath that poster are supporting documents, the challenge, prototype designs, supporting anchor charts, and inquiry questions. Our kids create a picture or project team index cards that show where that team is in the solution process. Teams or individuals move at their own pace through the stages. As each team progresses, the kids move their symbolic representation forward to match the stage. We support our learners as they move forward in the solution process as we differentiate

TABLE 6.4 Find a Solution through Bloom's

How Kids Go through the Stages to Find a Solution	
Learners Think through the Stages of Finding a Solution	**Teachers Design and Plan through the Revised Bloom's Taxonomy**
Stage 1: Authentic Challenge and Purpose How do we know if our kids understand the challenge?	Understanding
Stage 2: Information and Prototyping How do we know if our kids have created a viable prototype?	Applying
Stage 3: Perspective and Point of View How do we know if our kids have thought about different ideas?	Analyzing
Stage 4: Actions and Consequences How do we know if our kids have moved beyond their initial beliefs?	Evaluating
Stage 5: Considerations and Conclusions How do we know if our kids have reached the best possible solution for their audience?	Creating

Remembering is spiraled throughout the project

the instruction and scaffold for individuals, small groups, teams, or our whole class. Thus, not every team or every child is in the same stage at any given time and our children may move back and forth between Stage 2 and Stage 3, as needed. This is similar to a process with which you may already be familiar. The way a Pre-K child moves their clothes pin on the daily schedule is the same way that a Pre-K child is able to move their picture when they complete a stage. Where they are in the project is based on where they are in their thinking and prototype development. They are rewarded for thinking through a stage. Thus, there is a combination of small extrinsic rewards with a much larger dose of intrinsic motivation, as a stage is completed. Once a child or team has moved through a stage, they demonstrate a sense of confidence in their ability to move forward in the project and develop a sense of accomplishment and pride in their work.

As our learners visually see the results of their efforts via the stages, we establish a similar approach for our planning, using Bloom's Taxonomy, to ensure that our questions, lessons, and activities are aligned to their thinking. We recommend planning out two or three questions at each level to have handy, so you don't have to try and make them up on the fly. In our classrooms we used to keep the Bloom's Taxonomy verbs on the ceiling tiles so we could look up to grab the verbs that would help generate critical thinking questions at the right level.

During the Stages of Finding a Solution we allow our learners to begin with their own creative ideas and take ownership of their prototypes. It is important to reiterate this ownership through the project process as they continue to improve the quality of their solution. We reactivate their intrinsic motivation by using their own work. This is the way we identify and reinforce the value of their thinking. In simple terms, when our kids are given the opportunity to determine the answer to a problem, they acknowledge their feelings about it. They also get to choose what the product looks like and how it's presented. The results are intrinsically meaningful and memorable to them. This is why we want to focus on letting them ask the questions to which they want to find the answers. This stake in their learning goes a long way. Conversely, with a reliance on the extrinsic factor of being told what they need to learn, we find that motivation works in the short term, but not the long term. The extrinsic motivator becomes just another thing my teacher told me to do and eventually loses its value. Contrary to this, if we encourage the natural curiosity innate in our learners, we help to lead them to the discovery of the many questions they pose. In fact, some of the questions may not be ones that we initially considered and lead to higher quality thinking and solutions for our learners and our class.

The connection between high quality thinking and a high quality project requires our learners to take their thinking to a higher level. They must dig deeper to apply everything they researched and learned to create something. Therefore, the output of critical thinking is creativity. As we've noted previously, an authentic challenge starts with creation—the highest level of Bloom's Taxonomy. This requires our learners to move through each level of the taxonomy. If we ensure our authentic challenges are supported through each of the levels of Bloom's, we are more likely to see our children focus on the end goal: the creation level of the taxonomy. This means, the sometimes tedious and mundane lower levels of Bloom's are where kids frequently remain, because it is easier for teachers to instruct and assess at this level. When coupled with all the levels of Bloom's, the lower levels are now viewed as the building blocks of critical thinking. They define the path needed in order to successfully find a solution.

It is worth noting that it is easy to confuse intrinsic motivation with perseverance. Sustained inquiry is part of the critical thinking process, but sticking to a task doesn't necessarily mean that one is intrinsically motivated.

In order to have the motivation that comes from within, transformational learning must occur. In a Pre-K classroom, the sensory center is aligned to the challenge. In Pre-K and kindergarten, the dramatic play center includes a role play to help learners understand about the experts that may come to their classroom. From Pre-K to third grade, shared and interactive readings help our learners reflect on their solutions through the characters they are reading about. In later years, reciprocal reading and reflective journal responses help our children express what motivates them. A child that is empowered by the learning experience, through the ability to potentially effect change, is a child who embraces new challenges and reflects on them. These challenges are what foster the love of learning, reinforce a child's natural curiosity, and bring meaning to the hours and days spent inside a classroom. These challenges are at the highest level of Bloom's.

Learner Reflection

Reflection, in some capacity, comes naturally to kids. It is up to us to hone this skill and do so in such a way that we tie it to intrinsic motivation. As we model reflection techniques, we have the opportunity to turn reflection into an intrinsic motivator for learner growth. In fact, the incorporation of targeted reflection into the Stages of Finding a Solution is a good way for our children to maintain the intrinsic motivation we strive to cultivate. It is natural, as adults, to reflect on oneself in a negative way. We have all been there. "I should have done this." "If I had only done that." These are exactly the sentiments we want our learners to avoid.

It is really important that our kids complete a reflection of their learning, but what truly activates intrinsic motivation is when they do something with that reflection. It is not okay to just reflect. We have to get our kids to use their reflections to engage in meaningful dialogue in order to capitalize on their growth potential through those reflections. This is what motivates them to improve their work. This is when transformational learning happens. This is the shift from, "what I used to know" to "what I know now."

The use of predesigned reflection prompts is a good place to model for our children how to make reflection meaningful. Table 6.5 lists example prompts that do just that. Please adjust these as needed to ensure they are developmentally appropriate for the children in your classrooms. These questions focus on the satisfaction of learning to help amplify the intrinsic motivation within our kids. If we build in specific time into our daily routines and schedules for our kids to reflect on their work within the authentic challenge, we also build their capacity to enjoy learning.

TABLE 6.5 Reflection Prompts to Support Intrinsic Motivation

Stages of Finding a Solution	Possible Reflection Questions
Stage 1: Authentic Challenge and Purpose	• What information did I already know? • How can I use the information I already know?
Stage 2: Information and Prototyping	• What information did I enjoy learning about the most? • What worked well with my first prototype?
Stage 3: Perspective and Point of View	• How will I use what I learned from the expert? • How has my thinking changed for the better after listening to other ideas?
Stage 4: Actions and Consequences	• What positive contributions did I make to my team? • How have I grown as a learner during this challenge?
Stage 5: Considerations and Conclusions	• Why should I be proud of my final product? • How does my final product help others or my community?

These reflection prompts are also a built-in way for us to formatively assess the learning as it happens. Refer back to Table 5.1 for ideas on how to incorporate these prompts into your possible assessment activities. From the responses of our learners, we make adjustments to our instruction to support them as individuals and as teams. A focus on the positive reflections of their learning, coupled with the support we provide, helps to ensure the intrinsic motivation does not fade throughout a project. If anything, it aids in our measurement of a learner's sense of improvement. This is then easily tied to the goal setting that each child does.

Goal setting and reflection work in tandem. We like to start goal setting early on during our routines in the classroom. In fact, we introduce goal setting as early as the first day of class. When we ask our children what they explicitly want to gain, as learners, for the year, we immediately tap into the intrinsic motivation they have. Even our Pre-K and kindergarten kids have a lot to say about what they want. At this age, they have already developed their own personal opinions and values based on the prior experiences they bring into the classroom. Later, as our learners reflect during authentic challenges, and more specifically, during each Stage of Finding a Solution, they set new goals. Thus, in actuality, children help to determine their path for learning. If we continually act upon a child's intrinsic motivation by providing them their own path for learning, we get independent and motivated learners. This also creates a space for more individualized learning in the classroom. Remember, the key to authentic project-based learning design is to understand that our learners are not unmotivated. They are just motivated by different things.

We suggest that goal setting take several forms. For our youngest learners, it can be a simple conversation in which we prompt them to tell us what they like about school, what they don't like, what they can do to be a better learner, and what we can do to help them grow as learners. For older kids, a written plan for their goal and how they will accomplish it, with our help, is suggested. A written goal is more likely to be followed. It also has the ability to be connected with any of our reflection prompts from Table 6.5 above. As our learners reflect during each stage, have them note how well they have reached their goal. Adjustments can always be made and new goals set, when appropriate. In short, once children have a say in their learning plan, they are intrinsically motivated to follow it.

Homework and Motivation

It is often a struggle to get our children to complete homework, at any age. While many of our Pre-K kiddos are excited to bring something from home for show and tell, a few may actually become stressed at the thought of choosing just one thing. By the time we reach kindergarten, nightly reading and anchor word practice becomes the norm. First grade introduces the idea of spelling homework in preparation for a weekly test and a typical math worksheet is added into the mix. Homework in the second grade and beyond sometimes involves social studies or science activities and usually requires a biography, life events timeline, or other similar "project" for completion during off-school hours. How many kids actually do this homework on a regular basis and out of those that do, how many do it willingly?

We've found our own children, at home, vacillate between reasonable compliance and downright dread of homework completion. However, the fear of "owing five" during recess time is usually enough of an external motivating factor to get them moving for the 30–45 minutes it generally takes to complete it. But, what if we could tap into the intrinsic motivation that each of our children has to get them to eagerly complete homework and enjoy doing it? What if we could weave that intrinsic motivation together with the natural curiosity that our children have?

Let's think back to our Chapter 3 example on the weather emergency kits. Part of what prompted our idea to develop the project stemmed from a previous year's assignment. It was a more traditional homework assignment created by our friends at the local fire department. For fire safety prevention week, the kids were told to go home and create a map of their house. From that map, they had to determine the two best escape routes to take if a fire broke out. When we saw how anxious the kids were to talk to the parents about what they had learned and to develop something on their own, we knew we had to take it a step further.

This is why we also want you to think about what you assign for homework and how you expect your kids to benefit from it. What authentic problems can you use to replace the math traditional worksheets? For instance, when our learners were asked to create the map of their home and plot out their exit plan, they were also able to practice measurement and scale. This is the type of authentic homework that replaces worksheets. It is also the type of homework that motivates our children to continue their learning after the school day ends. Moreover, it provides another opportunity for kids to communicate what they are learning and why they are learning it.

As Chapter 4 has shown, we agree that literacy is an important component of all that we do. However, there are many different ways in which we can get our kids to read outside of class without making them feel as though the requirement is a punishment. While we certainly can rely on extrinsic motivation and rewards, such as filling out a monthly reading chart to exchange for a coupon to the local pizza shop, this does not necessarily build a love of reading. In fact, have you ever noticed that the children who complete these charts are actually the ones who love reading in the first place? They are otherwise intrinsically motivated to read. The pizza may just be a bonus. However, what motivated them in the beginning? Chances are that these children are already good readers. Children who struggle with reading are less likely to want to read for pleasure. Also these intrinsically motivated readers have probably found a genre of books they enjoy. Perhaps the "Magic Tree House" series allows them to escape into an alternate sense of reality. Maybe the "A to Z Mysteries" books abate their insatiable desire to solve mysteries. In any case, they want to read, because they have been given a choice as to what to read. Therefore, we need to find ways to activate the intrinsic motivation of all our readers and to do so in such a way that they read books related to the authentic challenge.

When our learners find the project to be both authentic and relevant to their lives, there is an increase in interest and enjoyment in the learning process. The same holds true for reading. Thus, once we tie our literacy components with our project challenge, we also see an increase in the interest of reading. This, however, does not mean we provide all of our children with the same books to read. We still must consider the appropriate reading levels for our kids. Additionally, we need to help our readers choose the appropriate books for their own consumption. Rather than allowing a child to pick a book that is too hard, even if it seems interesting to them, we want to guide them to a more appropriate reading level. Don't get us wrong, we highly encourage our own learners to challenge themselves and would rather them strive to read something too difficult than too easy. However, a move to more than one reading level above their identified one may easily lead to frustration and a shift back to extrinsic motivation.

Strategy Five promotes the social and emotional development of children who are eager and willing to learn. The activation of intrinsic motivation in our learners results in children who are proud of their accomplishments. Throughout each stage of the authentic challenge, they have contributed to their own development as critical thinkers, collaborators, and creative individuals. We have taught them to notice and appreciate the value of their thinking and contributions. Thus, we have allowed them to move beyond mere content memorization to play off of their natural curiosity. Our kids now notice how smart they are, which, in turn, builds their confidence and increases the likelihood that they will stay more intrinsically motivated throughout their academic career. What are your next steps? Reflect here, before you move onto the following chapter, on how to activate your learners' intrinsic motivations.

Where are You?
What are You Thinking?
How do You Feel?

Take Action	Seek Community	Think Aloud
Reflect on the authentic challenge you've been considering. List at least two ways in which your learners will be intrinsically motivated by the authentic challenge you have chosen.	Share your learners' motivations with a teaching partner and solicit feedback. Ask your partner to come up with two new ways in which they think your learners will be intrinsically motivated to complete the challenge you have chosen.	After reading this chapter, how has your thinking changed about what's intrinsically and extrinsically motivating for your learners? How did this chapter intrinsically motivate you to deepen your practice?

7

Language Learners: Projects and English Language and Dual Language Learners

How do I develop projects that improve language acquisition for my language learners?

Jose walked into second grade not knowing a word of English. He was scared and confused as the world around him buzzed with sounds and noises. He knew the voices were communication with words, but he could not keep up with the pace of any of the conversations. His teacher, Andrea, walked him to a seat and helped him get settled as she did for all of her children on the first day of school. By the end of the week, she knew Jose was in the preproduction phase of learning a new language. It would take at least six weeks and lots of images, pictures, charts, and visuals for Jose to begin to process his thoughts in English. Andrea had already decided to begin her first authentic challenge after the first week of school, but determined that Jose's participation in the challenge would make him feel more a part of the classroom community. The challenge was designed to bring the classroom, home, and family together. She wanted to build a classroom community that was bonded by their interests and daily experiences: "How can we create a classroom where everyone counts?"

As Andrea set up the challenge she chose a bilingual story book to read during her circle time. She read each page in English and in Spanish. She knew her Spanish was not great, but she gave it her best shot. When some of her kids laughed at her Spanish pronunciations she only responded with, "I feel proud that I tried." She then asked her kids what made them feel proud? She had them call out a few answers and then face each other and share one thing they were proud of accomplishing. For this activity, Andrea had purposely placed her learners in pairs so her ELL kids could discuss their thoughts in their first language. This afforded Jose the opportunity to be a part of the conversation and feel connected to the group. As a monolingual teacher, Andrea was accustomed to using translation tools to aid her as she worked with her ELL kids. When she solicited responses from her learners, they shared out an accomplishment that made them proud. She knew that capturing their accomplishments on paper would be a good writing experience for her learners. She placed one kid volunteer to the left of her, to write the words in the target language (English). Another kid volunteer was to the right of her, trying their best to write words in their first language (Spanish). One child had enough command of the English language to share out for the both of them. This was the start of a project that opened the door for kids like Jose to share who they were and about their culture. This was also an opportunity for these children to feel connected to the other kids, while the whole class began their journey of developing a classroom community based on trust. The project also helped Andrea's English Language Learners to increase their vocabulary acquisition, make meaning of words, and engage with the language.

How do I develop projects that improve language acquisition for my language learners? An authentic project supports the children like Jose in our classrooms, as they acquire new skills in reading, writing, and conversation. It also supports their ability and agility to use their new vocabulary in their daily experiences. The inquiry process, or process of answering questions, at the creation level provides an even deeper foundation to support the acquisition and mastery of language. When our learners are first introduced to their authentic challenge, which is written at the highest level of Bloom's, they automatically shed light on their prior content knowledge and experiences by the questions they ask about the challenge. Remember, a lack of questions is to be expected from all of our learners and not just our second language learners. This is sometimes merely an indication that they are thinking. We do not need to fill the silence with our own questions, but rather afford them the time to process the challenge. The authentic challenge appeals to our learners' natural tendencies to want to solve problems, complete puzzles, and design something on their own. This is the perfect chance to tell our children they have the creative freedom to come up with their own ideas. This is especially attractive to our second language learners, as they now have a purpose and reason to use the language, rather than simply the requirement of language use for the completion of a worksheet.

> **Take Note**: Both English Language Learners and Dual Language Learners benefit from the strategies we have included in this chapter. However, don't hesitate to use these tools for any of your learners, as all children have unique needs in the classroom. Part of the beauty of a project-based learning experience is the freedom it provides us to scaffold when and as needed. Our goal, overall and with all of our learners, is to ensure our learners improve in their use of academic language or the vocabulary and grammar needed to successfully participate in and out of school.

Helpful Background on Language Acquisition

Our goal is to combine all of the good instructional strategies that we already use with our young learners and partner them with their natural curiosity and love for learning. We want them to find creative and innovative solutions where they take their own ideas and turn them into viable products they present to a public audience. However, specific training in how to support English Language Learners, dual language kids, and bilingual children is typically focused on the acquisition of language through direct instruction and targeted strategies and activities. The use of authentic learning, project-based learning, and hands-on activities is the key to enable our children to generate spoken, read, and written language. We find a lot of hands-on activities, activity workshops, pre-made and presold materials, and websites with multiple strategies that claim to get language learners to produce language. We want to arm you with the tools needed to authentically engage our Dual Language Learners. You may have only a few English Language Learners in your classroom or you may have many. You may be a bilingual educator or a dual language educator. Whatever your classroom situation, we know that certain cultural norms guide its structure. Our learners need explicit and targeted instruction in vocabulary, as well as consistent and frequent opportunities to talk, reflect, and work with peers and experts. Coupled together, these produce frequent interactions with the language, rich language inputs, routine scaffolding from the teacher, and continued development of the home language. The use of authentic challenges and project-based learning does not mean that phonics, phonological awareness, and print awareness go by the wayside. In fact, they are a pivotal piece that, when integrated with an authentic challenge, motivates our learners to use the target language in a more meaningful and effective way. Therefore, our direct instruction opportunities still have a place in our second language learners' day as they are working on a challenge. However, it is the challenge that makes the vocabulary come to life, gives the reading a purpose, and gives pictures and words a reason for being on the paper. Any second language learner needs targeted language support and strategies to help them hear the language being modeled. They also need opportunities to practice that modeled language in various authentic settings and in repeated ways. This is the first step to begin using the language in a functional way.

In early childhood education we have the opportunity to begin the language acquisition process at a time when our learners' brains are building the literacy constructs that will make up their lifelong schema. Our learners combine their background knowledge with every new piece of information they encounter during their day. Every reading, writing, and speaking experience deepens their existing knowledge and builds new knowledge to support their success in the target language. Extensive opportunities to practice vocabulary and reading expand their language acquisition rate and increase their ability to use the language. This language use manifests first in a conversational way and then develops into a more formal manner. This is something of which we need to remain mindful, as we engage our second language learners in authentic project-based learning experiences.

In order to fully understand how our second language learners function in the classroom, we need to comprehend how our learners converse in their own homes. Translanguaging is commonplace for many of our ELL kids and even with our children who are learning in a dual language school. This is also known as a type of code switching. Many children do it at home, even if their parents prefer to or only speak their native language. One person may speak one language while the other responds in the second language. This happens because our brain does not think in one language at a time as we learn another language. The brain does not have an English side and a Spanish side. Therefore, translanguaging is the opportunity to take risks with a few of the words that are known well and the words that are used frequently. Through interactive experiences within the classroom, we want our second language learners to move to a space in which they feel comfortable with the use of the dominant language in the classroom, as they improve their fluency and proficiency with their second language acquisition.

An authentic challenge promotes the role of oral language proficiency through repeated collaborative conversations. This proficiency has a huge impact on reading and math achievement, over time. Therefore, the key to good project design is to make sure we embed enough opportunities for our learners to use academic language in real time with real outcomes. The more robust their oral language and vocabulary is, the greater the correlation is to improved reading fluency and reading comprehension. For example, in our weather unit from Chapters 2 and 3, we introduced the project words of the week. They were not the expected CVC or CVCC (consonant/vowel/consonant/consonant) words, but the much larger words related to the project, such as precipitation, meteorology, and hurricanes. We made sure to explicitly create time for our kids to experience a nonfiction read-aloud about hurricanes and discuss hurricanes throughout the day. We used the word hurricane for our transitions, we drew hurricanes, and then we used the words in our centers alongside our CVC and CVCC words that we needed to practice. These project words became cumulative, over time. This authentic approach to vocabulary helps to increase a learner's level of understanding; at the same time it adds words connected to their challenge.

Scaffolding for Language Learners

Authentic projects provide the opportunity to stimulate the natural curiosity in our English Language and Dual Language Learners. This happens through an authentic challenge that is relevant to their lives. Authentic projects also give them the chance to solve challenges through the acquisition of new vocabulary and new knowledge via rich literacy experiences, connections to the community, and opportunities to be creative and innovative. This is true for both English Language Learners and learners in dual language classrooms. In both cases, our goal with our second language learners is to get them into a space where they engage academically in either their target or second language. They then are able to articulate the learned knowledge through the development of viable solutions to the authentic challenge. This approach brings the target language to life, as it is used in a relevant way, rather than through the use of arbitrary worksheets, memorized definitions, and other contrived situations.

In Chapter 4, we focused on successful literacy strategies for project-based classrooms that promote authentic and relevant work. Authentic projects have the ability to increase language acquisition levels by bringing together the concrete language work and the contextualized learning to bridge the divide and encourage deeper learning. Vocabulary and comprehension skills improve when we know which supports are needed within the various Stages of Finding a Solution. We support our language learners by providing targeted and directed scaffolds and assessments.

The ability to scaffold and assess our children at their language production levels is an important key to help them move through their design work. The success of the authentic challenge for a language learner is dependent upon the level of language scaffolding that our learners need during the implementation of our projects. This means each child may need different scaffolds in place to support their current language proficiency. This level of scaffolding and the type of strategies needed are also dependent on our type of classroom environment. The design of collaborative work encourages our learners to use both their target language and their first language as supports for their reading and listening abilities.

It is important that we don't overlook the abilities of our learners just because they don't have full language capabilities. Remember, all kids have natural curiosity and it is important to tap into this even when we are focused on second language learners. We don't want to assume that they need to stay in the lower levels of Bloom's just because their language acquisition isn't at full capacity.

Through the scaffolds we create via Bloom's Taxonomy, we may ask a certain question to a native speaker, but our second language learner most likely needs additional questions or simplified questions. We provide an example of this in Table 7.1, taken from our Pre-K project on the use of basic elements of shape to teach handwriting from Chapter 3. Nonetheless, we know that some of our second language learners may need even more supports. For our beginner language learners, we suggest the additional use of visual tools to enhance the meaning of the questions we ask. First, we ask the question, but also have the image ready to use, if needed. The picture provides the opportunity for our learners to make inferences based on the visual. However, it is okay if they experience a bit of productive struggle. This tactic works well with both our ELL children and our dual language program participants, as it is important to remember that part of the challenge, itself, is that they should not know the answer to the question right away. The same holds true for our first language learners, so we need to remember that while our second language learners have an additional obstacle to overcome, we do not want to provide them with too much information up front; we want them to uncover the meaning of the word. As the project ends, they have crafted a definition within the context of the academic language that has more meaning for them and is more likely to be fluently used in conversation.

TABLE 7.1 Bloom's Questions for Language Learners

Bloom's Taxonomy	First Level Language	Second Level Language
Creating	How do we curate our school like a museum?	How do we choose which pictures hang on the wall? • Touch the wall • Provide an empty picture frame • Show pictures of museum exhibits
Evaluating	How well did I include the elements of shape?	What is the best part of your picture? • Identify and point to a basic element of shape in a peer's drawing • Match the elements of shape to portions of the drawn picture
Analyzing	How does the first draft of my picture compare to the second draft of my picture?	How is my first picture different from my second picture? • Point to the same area of the two different pictures • Show a series of the same picture in several different stages of completion
Understanding	How do I draw a picture of myself?	What do I look like? • Show a picture of a kid-drawn portrait • Provide famous artist self-portraits for children to look through
Remembering	What is a museum?	Where is a place that we keep special things that we don't want people to touch? • Take a virtual tour of a museum • Provide piles of drawing materials

Through a targeted use of questioning, based on the levels of Bloom's, we foster a classroom culture of communication. As we model questioning, we also encourage our learners to question one another. This questioning process is not reserved for our first language learners. In a dual language classroom, as well as with our ELL kids, our questioning must not remain in the lower levels of Bloom's. While is it important that our children know and understand basic content and be able to converse using academic language, it is perfectly acceptable to have that conversation be full of flaws. Rather than spend the bulk of our time focused on the correction of grammar and pronunciation, we create the space to encourage our learners to share a sense of discovery as they question their peers, ask for additional explanations, and explore differing points of view. The more our ELL kids hear the language spoken, in this manner, the more they understand the types of conversation they are expected to produce. This also holds true for our Dual Language Learners, as they make their own sense and meaning of the content through the conversations they have with one another and through the guided conversations initiated by us.

It can be difficult to intentionally shift the amount of time we generally spend talking during any given day. As teachers, we are sometimes apt to feel like we need to talk and to do so especially when our kids appear to be struggling. However, it is necessary to make the shift if we want to ensure our learners practice their language skills, as well as spend a great deal of their time deep in the inquiry process. If we switch the percentage of time that we spend talking with of the percentage of time that our learners speak, amazing results are produced. For this, we generally like to stick with the 80/20 rule. If we only spend 20 percent of our time talking, compared to the 80 percent that we encourage our kids to speak, we are personally challenged to choose our words carefully. We may choose to use this 20 percent time for questioning through the levels of Bloom's or to provide strategic feedback on any given Stage of Finding a Solution. If we spend our 20 percent time asking our learners to focus on rote memorization only, our learners are not using their academic language to the point of proficiency and beyond. It is only through the real use of conversation that our kids become proficient in the use of the language.

While we may need to model the conversation process, the longer our second language learners spend involved in solving an authentic challenge, the more we want to pass the responsibility of initiating the conversation to them. Part of the benefit of a project-based learning approach is the ownership it encourages for our learners. Therefore, we also want our second language learners to start and to own their conversations. As they get deeper into the inquiry process, they are automatically placed in a position where they have to ask questions, respond to inquiries, and provide feedback. This also pushes our learners to think critically about an authentic and relevant challenge.

Throughout the conversation process, we encourage our learners to look to one another for affirmation, rather than to us. While it is more than acceptable to nod our head or say something similar to "That's an interesting idea," we have to resist the urge to correct or direct the conversation. If we dedicate too much time to correcting grammar, we don't guide our learners to the higher levels of Bloom's. If we spend more time interrupting their thoughts, they aren't able to finish those thoughts to move into the next Stage of Finding a Solution. Instead, we use our notes about these conversations as formative assessments to determine further supports that we may want to implement during the Stages of Finding a Solution.

Support through the Stages of Finding a Solution

During each Stage of Finding a Solution, we provide linguistically accommodated content-based instruction and targeted language scaffolds to support our second language learners. The stages provide the entry points for language usage accommodations and strategies. Within and throughout the project, separate content assessments and language assessments help our learners understand their successes and discuss their areas of growth. Please use the tools that work best for you and your learners. We have listed several options you may want to explore in Table 7.2. Feel free to incorporate these strategies with any of your learners, as well. While they are good for target language scaffolds, differentiating for any and all children with these tools adds an additional layer of support when and if needed.

TABLE 7.2 Authentic Challenge and Purpose

Stage of Finding a Solution	Target Language Scaffolding Tools
Stage 1: Authentic Challenge and Purpose How do we know if our kids understand the challenge and why they are doing it?	• Cognitive Content Dictionary (GLAD) • Active Reading Guides and Choral Reading • Use visuals and have learners point to pictures or act out vocabulary • Single Bubble Map • Bilingual and picture dictionary • Frayer Model/Four Box Vocabulary • I Know/You Know with sentence frames • Inside Outside Circles • Three-Step Interview • GRASPS

As our first stage focuses on the start of the project, we must ensure all of our learners are clear as to what the challenge asks of them. This is especially important for our second language learners. Words are easily lost in translation or a simple misinterpretation of the word potentially throws the entire challenge into an experience of frustration. Some of the scaffolding tools we have listed, in this stage and the others, are commonly referenced as GLAD (Guided Language Acquisition Design) strategies. The GLAD Project, developed by the Orange County Department of Education in Los Angeles, was developed to ensure English Language Learners are not segregated from their grade-level peers, but rather integrated into the mainstream classroom. Their focus is to increase the academic language that we have discussed at multiple points in this chapter. While they have 35 activities for ELL support, we specifically note the ones we suggest for authentic project-based learning. Feel free to explore their other resources and utilize them as desired and when appropriate.

The GLAD Cognitive Content Dictionary is a favorite of ours. Not only do our children predict the definition of the given vocabulary word through context clues, but they also create a visual representation of the word. This is especially helpful if a word is used in our challenge question that is unfamiliar to our learners. Similarly, the mere action of physically demonstrating the meaning of a word helps a child to better grasp the meaning of it. The use of picture dictionaries is also helpful at this stage for the same reasons. To visualize a word is a concrete action that helps to give the word life.

Partner work in this stage, as in all stages, helps to increase the conversational dialogue that takes place. It also requires our children to look at each other as resources and leaders in the classroom, instead of the focus on you, the teacher, as the leader. An "I Know/You Know" activity with sentence frames is an easy way to begin the partner work. The Inside-Outside Circle and the Three-Step Interview, both Kagan strategies, are beneficial to our learners as they require deep conversation. They help to produce the questioning environment we discussed earlier in this chapter and get our kids started in the inquiry process as they develop questions they need to answer about the challenge. The use of graphic organizers has the same potential here. We might choose to use a single bubble map where our learners discuss the challenge and then add details with words or short sentences. A Frayer Model or Four Box Vocabulary provides a similar approach for organization of initial ideas and thoughts about the challenge. For our Pre-K kids, we want to focus more on the observation of their actions and take low inference anecdotal notes. We take low inference notes as they address very specific behaviors and observations. All subjectivity and value judgments are removed so we focus more on their peer-to-peer interactions and acquisition of vocabulary. How they respond to their peers while using these strategies informs our instructional planning and helps us to respond to their learning needs.

To support the active nature of our young learners, we tap into their kinesthetic side with a few of the scaffolds. We want to go beyond the simple use of visuals to make connections and ask our kids to point to related pictures and then act out the vocabulary terms. Similar to a game of charades, it bridges the gap between fluency levels. Active reading guides and choral reading, while not as physically active, do require more than passive listening. Here, it is helpful if we model pronunciations, while alleviating the pressure of the spotlight on any one child as they struggle with appropriate inflections.

If we find our second language learners struggle with the challenge and what needs to be accomplished in order to do it, we utilize a modified GRASPS form. The GRASPS approach, developed by Wiggins and McTighe (2004), is an Understanding by Design concept that asks learners to identify the goal, role, audience, situation, product, and standards for the challenge. As we break down these components through targeted questions, our learners break down their thought processes into more manageable chunks. Thus, an even more modified format of the GRASPS approach is helpful for second language learners. Whether you use this approach or any of the other scaffolds we have mentioned, the goal is to ensure your learners and you encapsulate several points.

- ◆ **Your Learners**: Understand the reason for the challenge
- ◆ **You**: Document their awareness of their role within the project to gauge their understanding of it
- ◆ **Your Learners**: Know what they are supposed to do in the challenge
- ◆ **You**: Provide time for them to articulate the purpose of the challenge so they can orally explain why they are doing the project
- ◆ **Your Learners**: Know what job they must complete for the challenge
- ◆ **You**: Keep track of the completion of their assigned tasks to ensure they don't fall behind and become frustrated

In our Information and Prototyping stage, our learners are at the start of deep levels of gathering details, data, and content. This may be more than overwhelming for our second language learners, so it is necessary to plan for the appropriate supports. Table 7.3 lists a variety of options for you to review. Videos shown in both the first and second language are a good place to start. BrainPop Jr. currently offers online videos in Spanish and in French, but they also have a specially designed series for English Language Learners. The visuals, combined with the content specific vocabulary, reinforce our focus on an authentic conversational approach related to the authentic challenge. These visuals are also implemented through picture cards or finger puppet activities in which our kids use the puppets to act out vocabulary terms.

Through the use of knowledge inventories, our learners retell stories or experiences. We, or another child, are able to write down the narratives for our second language learners to take home to read. This is a simple way to reinforce their learning. This use of the first language and target language is similar to the Scan for Vocabulary tool that adds words and their meanings in the first language and then compares it in the second language. It is also a perfect place to use context clues, picture clues, and a search for cognates. The Narrative Input Chart also uses pictures in conjunction with words. Here, we use a picture that portrays the information and on the back of the picture, the words, sentences, and paragraphs describe the picture. This scaffold also reinforces the visual connection between the information and the conversational aspect of the challenge.

Graphic organizers are a helpful tool as our learners make sense of the information they have gathered. It is also imperative for our kids to put down as much information as possible. This means they might need

TABLE 7.3 Information and Prototyping

Stage of Finding a Solution	Target Language Scaffolding Tools
Stage 2: Information and Prototyping How do we know if our kids have created a viable product?	• Knowledge Inventories • Listen to videos in both first and second language • Narrative Input Chart (GLAD) • Dramatic Play/Block Center/Finger Puppet Activities • Picture Cards • Open-Narrow-Close • Interactive Drawing Journal • Scribing Sessions • Scan for Vocabulary Tool • Tree Maps

to draw some of their information, as they work toward making meaning of the content. This reinforces their understanding of the vocabulary. We scribe, as needed, or assign a partner to facilitate the scribing process. All of these tools assist our learners as they make connections between the content and any prototypes they need to make. As they make their prototypes, we continue to ask them to reflect on that process as well. By the end of this stage, all first and second language learners need to have completed several components with our help and support.

◆ **Your Learners**: Collect helpful information through active learning
◆ **You**: Provide hands-on activities and opportunities for reading/read-alouds
◆ **Your Learners**: Use their gathered data in a meaningful way
◆ **You**: Structure experiences that require them to apply data
◆ **Your Learners**: Create two or more drafts of a final product
◆ **You**: Formatively assess each draft and provide meaning feedback

---

The consideration of others' perspectives and points of view may seem intimidating to a second language learner. As they struggle to make their own sense of the content used to support their quest to find a solution to the challenge, they may become overwhelmed at the prospect of others' ideas. As we build in supports to make the transition into this stage, we can consider a multitude of options. Once again, we turn to several time-tested GLAD strategies for this stage. Table 7.4 lists several of these strategies we have found to be successful. Team Tasks calls for us to model a strategy and then revisit it a minimum of one additional time before learner groups tackle the same task. Then, the task is charted as a group before the learner completes it on an individual basis. The mere scaffold of a teacher model first and a group assignment second, before we turn it over to our second language learners to complete, greatly improves the likelihood of a sense of accomplishment. Similarly, Story Maps provides a model for our learners through the act of reading a story that has a clear problem and solution. In the Story Map, our class first charts the challenge faced by the characters in the story. Then, they list all of the sequential actions taken that lead up to the resolution of the problem. Thus, our kids are able to see not only the sequence that takes place

TABLE 7.4 Perspective and Point of View

Stage of Finding a Solution	Target Language Scaffolding Tools
Stage 3: Perspective and Point of View How do we know if our kids have thought about different ideas?	• Reciprocal Teaching • Roving Reporter • Author Study • Anchor Charts • Comparative Input Chart (GLAD) • Role Play • Conversation Station • Scenarios • Story Maps (GLAD) • Team Tasks (GLAD)

when a problem is solved, but they also encounter the actions of those involved in the story and any points of view considered before the challenge comes to a resolution. It provides an opportunity for our learners to apply the same type of thinking to their own challenge as they consider the ideas of others. It also gives them more confidence if they are required to interact with an expert on the challenge. Finally, the Comparative Input Chart, also from GLAD, gives learners the chance to use a pictorial form of a Venn diagram to compare the different points of view.

There are several additional model-type strategies that effectively anchor our second language learners' discussions in the advanced nuances of our conversational techniques. Through the use of a role play, in this stage, we provide our learners with scenarios that represent a variety of points of view. This gives our kids the opportunity to articulate themselves, in a practice setting, through the use of academic language. The use of scenarios is very similar, but encourages our kids to practice this academic language in written format or, if they are emerging writers, it is dictated in a scribing session. A conversation station presents the occasion to hold a microphone and practice the use of academic language. The mere act of recording and listening to that recording helps our second language learners to pick up on pronunciations and key details they may otherwise miss. Even in our morning meetings we provide the chance for our learners to run the discussion. In this case, they model the physical response of the language the entire time, rather than participate passively.

Often second language learners feel more comfortable working with their peers than with adults. They relate to one another in a way that they may find more difficult with us. The use of reciprocal teaching gives open-ended questions for discussion in a small group setting and gives them the opportunity to interact with their peers in a structured manner. This lessens the stress that a language learner might feel and decreases the potential for confusion that may occur without guided questions provided. The use of a roving reporter format encourages reflective thinking and conversational interaction between our kids. It also gives our language learners a sense of purpose and importance in the classroom. An author study asks our learners to make connections between their own life and the characters in a story or the author's life. For our English Language Learners, we suggest the use of Julie Cummin's *Country Kid, City Kid*. The wonderful illustrations and easy to read text give our language learners the opportunity to practice determining differing points of view based on the characters' experiences and places they live. Finally, the use of anchor or brain growth charts provides an opportunity for our learners to list new information in order to make sense of it. This is a great place for them to record information learned from experts with whom they may interact. All of the scaffolds for this stage ensure multiple points for our language learners to exhibit their understanding and uncover any difficulties they may have that require further supports.

- ◆ **Your Learners**: Talk to experts
- ◆ **You**: Find experts who can relate to young kids
- ◆ **Your Learners**: Provide and receive peer feedback
- ◆ **You**: Build time into your schedule to have feedback opportunities
- ◆ **Your Learners**: Reflect on their project throughout the process
- ◆ **You**: Incorporate reflection prompts into journaling, kid writing, or scribing sessions

---

The actions and consequences stage has the potential to be a frustrating one for our second language learners. They may have difficulty communicating even the subtlest differences in the ways in which their beliefs about the challenge have changed over the course of the project. At this stage, our scaffolds are designed to support them in their quest to communicate these differences, why they made changes to their prototypes, and the consequences of those differences. Here, we once again utilize several GLAD strategies that you will find listed in Table 7.5.

TABLE 7.5 Actions and Consequences

Stage of Finding a Solution	Target Language Scaffolding Tools
Stage 4: Actions and Consequences How do we know if our kids have moved beyond their initial beliefs?	• Co-op Strip Paragraph • Process Grid (GLAD) • Think it Through • Experts "In the House" • Café Conversations • Pyramid Teaching • Learning Logs • Agreement Circles • SCAMPER • Observation Charts (GLAD)

The Process Grid, designed to help with expository text writing, asks our learners to categorize information. The breakdown of this information into categories helps our kids to segment their thinking, thus lessening the overwhelming feeling of trying to output too much information at once. While GLAD generally calls for the use of Process Grids to work with basic information, in this stage we ask for deeper critical thinking. Categories we like to incorporate in this activity include steps taken during the project and the results of those actions. We also incorporate the use of pictorials and narratives to complete the Process Grid. Similarly, our use of GLAD's Observation Charts digs deeper into inquiry process. For this, we need to plan ahead, as our learners must take pictures of the work that they do during the project process. The pictures are then used to spur a deeper insight into the thoughts of our second language learners and provide us a window into what additional supports we may need to implement for their success. As our kids show us the pictures they have taken, they write an observation of the work they were doing at that particular time. We also have them ask a question about the picture. This question is what definitively helps us in our formative assessment of their needs. The pictures also provide a growth chart of the learning that has occurred.

Agreement circles help our learners to reassess their own thinking about the challenge. First, we place our learners in a circle and then simply provide a statement: all kids who agree with the statement must enter the center of the circle; if they disagree they stay on the outside of the circle. A discussion ensues between a pair of kids that represent one learner who agrees with the statement and one who does not. The process repeats with a follow-up statement. Our second language learners are able to take in the conversation from their partner and process the information in a more controlled setting. They are more likely to feel safe in this type of smaller debate setting than they would in a much larger one. Café Conversations, Think it Through, and Experts "In the House" are variations on activities with the same end goal. Small group conversations provide a safe space for our learners to communicate about the actions and consequences that their product will have on the people, places, and things in their learning community and beyond.

Learning logs are the most basic way to get our learners to communicate the actions they take and the consequences that may result from those actions. We suggest the implementation of these early on in the project process. Here, however, you really want their focus to be more about "if this … then that …", rather than a simple "this is what I accomplished" approach. Alternatively, a collaborative approach to the actions and consequences stage is to implement a twist on the cooperative strip paragraph. For this, we generate what the actions are and our learners pick the consequences. This is a nice scaffold as we model the process before allowing our kids to try it on their own.

SCAMPER is designed to have our learners refine the work that they have completed thus far in the project. While it is a fabulous way to engage all of our learners in deeper thinking about their own ideas, it is especially helpful for our second language learners as they answer targeted questions, rather than provide a broad overview. In this process, we ask our kids to substitute, combine, adapt, modify, put to another use, eliminate, and reverse. All of these pieces focus on the requirement to take a specific action, such as substitute, and then determine the consequence of that action. Whether you use SCAMPER, one of the other scaffolds we have described in this stage, or combine the use of multiple scaffolds, ensure your second language learners have fully thought through the actions they have taken during the challenge and the consequences of those actions.

Pyramid Teaching is a combination of several segments of time designed to create a process for the thinking that your learners do through this phase of a project. Children either write about or draw representations of their ideas and possible solutions to the challenge. A scheduled meeting with individuals or small groups of kids gives you the opportunity to review their ideas and have them articulate their thinking. This then provides a deliberate space for your learners to make changes to their ideas in a reflective way in which they provide justifications for the intended changes.

> ◆ **Your Learners**: Kept a record of their ideas and solutions
> ◆ **You**: Create a process for them to follow to chart their ideas and solutions either through writing or drawing
> ◆ **Your Learners**: Understand the potential impact of their solutions
> ◆ **You**: Schedule discussions with small groups or individual kids
> ◆ **Your Learners**: Made reflective changes throughout the project
> ◆ **You**: Require them to make justifications for changes made

As our second language learners enter the final stage of their authentic challenge, it is time to enact several opportunities, some of which are listed in Table 7.6, for them to practice their presentations. While this is certainly important for all children, a second language learner finds this to be all the more imperative to calm nerves, work out any pronunciation kinks, and to feel comfortable with any and all visual materials they plan to incorporate in the presentation. If we don't realize the complexity and difficulty that second language learners have in acquiring cognitive academic language proficiency, a child's language ability can easily be over-estimated. Presentation practice provides another opportunity to demonstrate their cognitive academic language proficiency. Both the audience role-play scenario and the video presentation review are a good use of time in the waning days of the project. The role play presents our learners with possible roadblocks they may encounter during the presentation, while the video review gives them the opportunity to watch themselves present. This means they are able to practice their oral language fluency skills repeatedly, add missing pieces to the presentation, or recognize any idiosyncrasies they may exhibit.

TABLE 7.6 Considerations and Conclusions

Stage of Finding a Solution	Target Language Scaffolding Tools
Stage 5: Considerations and Conclusions How do we know if our kids have reached the best possible solution for their audience?	• Central Idea Diagram • SWOT Analysis (Good, Grow, Possible, Buggy) • Spider Web Discussion • Socratic Seminar • Mind Maps • Story Map (GLAD) • Text Clue Conclusion Group • Frame-by-Frame Approach • Video Presentation Review • Audience Role-Play Scenarios

Before we launch into the final presentation practice opportunities, we want to provide several other opportunities for scaffolds for the considerations and conclusions stage. The use of the previously discussed spider web discussion and Socratic Seminar provide plenty of opportunities for our learners to carry on a conversation. These conversations are targeted to further define and develop their final solutions and provide our second language learners an additional chance to feel confident in their conclusions. This is also true of the SWOT analysis, even though it does not create a space for a formal conversation. It does, however, target specifics, rather than generalize—an important scaffold for our language learners.

It is important for all kids to make connections between what they are learning and what is real to them. This is even more vital for our children who are working to acquire a second language. The use of the text conclusion group provides us with an opportunity to support this connection. In this activity, learners read a text and make any personal connections they may have with the text. It may be an experience they have had, a song they have heard, or a television show they have watched. This connection builds a cognitive schema for the learner. However, we know that some children may make more connections to the text than others. Thus, the second portion of this activity is vital. The teacher maps the connections listed by each child and once all connections are shared, the learners work together to find patterns that may emerge. These emergent patterns are used to reflect on possible solutions to the overall authentic challenge.

A central idea diagram or mind map also benefits our second language learners as they complete the organization of their final solutions. Similarly, the frame-by-frame approach we described in Chapter 5 is a simplified way for our learners to express their opinions and decisions as they near the completion of their final solution. As our learners near the end of this final stage, it is important to ensure that we have supported them as much as possible.

- ◆ **Your Learners**: Compared and contrasted their solution ideas
- ◆ **You**: Use visuals such as Venn diagrams for ease of comparison
- ◆ **Your Learners**: Put into words why a possible solution would not work
- ◆ **You**: Ask probing questions to get them to fully explain why a solution does not work
- ◆ **Your Learners**: Explained why they picked one solution over all others
- ◆ **You**: Provide the opportunity for them to articulate their solution to an authentic audience

As we feel more comfortable supporting our second language learners in authentic project-based learning, we need to keep a few things in mind. According to the Center for Advanced Research on Language Acquisition (CARLA), we are tasked with helping them to construct knowledge, develop understandings about a topic, use language meaningfully and purposefully, and learn about the language by actually using it. As you move forward in your own journey to incorporate more authentic learning experiences for your second language learners, what are your next steps? Reflect here, before you move on to the following chapter, on how you intend to support them in their journey to become more proficient in their target language.

Where are You?
What are You Thinking?
How do You Feel?

Take Action	Seek Community	Think Aloud
Choose two or three language strategies that you do not already use in your classroom. Connect the strategies to your everyday lesson planning and determine how they can impact your learners' comprehension and academic language proficiency.	Share your ideas with a teaching partner and solicit feedback on how you will impact your language learners' language proficiency using authentic project-based learning. Be sure to discuss the specific supports you intend to implement in order to help your second language learners be successful in the challenge.	What do you now know about supporting language learners and their academic proficiency levels that you didn't know before you read this chapter? How can you use the supports for all of your kids as they engage in an authentic challenge?

8

Communication, Collaboration, Critical Thinking, and Creativity

How do we create the space for communication, collaboration, critical thinking, and creativity to bolster our kids' natural curiosity?

We have spent the entirety of this book weaving in the components of the big four when it comes to twenty-first-century skills. Now, we want to take the time to explicitly connect them to the Stages of Finding a Solution. The folks at Partnership for 21st Century Learning (P21) have invested a lot of time and research on how to ensure our learners are college and career ready by the time they leave our charge. This includes our youngest learners, as they note, "At early ages, children's curiosity and intrinsic motivation make them highly receptive to experiences that build creative, collaborative, critical thinking and communication skills." Thus, it is important to keep in mind that our twenty-first-century classroom is based on more than just the need to carry out procedures focused on retrieved knowledge and the construction of models about what has been memorized. It is about relevant, real-world challenges that guide our learners through every level of Bloom's Taxonomy as they consistently and repeatedly employ collaboration, communication, critical thinking, and creativity to solve the challenge. The demonstration of all four components provides us with assessment opportunities of their social and emotional development and thinking skills, as well as their content knowledge. The inputs that build collaboration, communication, and critical thinking lead to the single most important output in authentic project-based learning: our learners' creativity. Therefore, we must ensure they engage deeply with each skill at all of the stages of finding their own solutions.

How do we create the space for communication, collaboration, critical thinking, and creativity to bolster our kids' natural curiosity? When we present our learners with ill-defined or fuzzy challenges, we provide them with the opportunity to personally define those challenges. As we ask our young learners to define problems and find their own solutions we tap into their natural curiosity. Our first role, in the process, is to design an open-ended project that immediately invites our kids to actively participate in the challenge. To do so, we must leverage our learners' intrinsic motivation through connections we help them to identify. Most notably, this includes their prior knowledge and how it connects to their engagement of newly introduced information. The ways in which our learners take apart, reorganize, and rearrange the information and materials we provide sets them up for early successes in the challenge. In the same way our learners physically take apart the materials we provide, they must also mentally take apart their cognitive models. Every new experience changes their thinking. With each additional project, we increase the schema and mental models of our learners as we foster this construction and deconstruction. In the beginning, this occurs through uninhibited play and hands-on activities. Our role as facilitators is to watch and observe, to listen, and take notes. We remain on the sidelines to encourage our learners to collaborate and communicate. To illustrate this process, let's refer back to our Pre-K art and handwriting project from Chapter 3. We began with a pile of art books, art materials, picture frames, and modeling clay. We provided no instruction to our learners, other than to tell them to move around the room and play with what we provided. We took video of our kids for the first 20 minutes as they moved around to the different items, engaged in natural dialogue and questioning, and manipulated the art items in various ways. We asked our kids to share their thinking about their play. What did they like? With what items had they previously played? What did they create? Where had they previously seen these items? A thinking map of their answers was created to capture their thinking and make it visible. As we recorded their dialogue, our learners were provided with an initial opportunity to collaborate with each other. This was used for an assessment of prior knowledge. Our learners had to think critically to connect their prior knowledge and personal experiences to the materials we introduced. These ideas were then shared with the class. All of these activities took place before the challenge was explained. As we first engaged our learners' natural curiosity, we intentionally set the stage for our kids to think creatively about the challenge. Yet, our young learners did not overtly experience anything except the enjoyment of play, spurred through the natural curiosity they possess. This is the type of learner engagement that is cyclical throughout each Stage of Finding a Solution. Our five strategies, presented in the previous chapters of this book, help you to plan for each stage as you deepen your learners' skills in critical thinking, communication, collaboration, and creativity. Table 8.1 details the relationship between these twenty-first-century skills and your learners, as well as your role in bolstering these skills.

Young learners use their natural curiosity to seek understanding. That natural curiosity is fostered in the areas of creativity, critical thinking, communication, and collaboration. As our learners engage in an authentic challenge, they constantly use these skills to meet their needs and to find solutions as they make sense of the world around them. Our deliberate inclusion of the four Cs is an iterative and cyclical process. Therefore, it is necessary to include each of them in all of the Stages of Finding a Solution.

TABLE 8.1 The Twenty-First-Century Skill Link

Learner	Twenty-First-Century Skills	Teacher
Personalized learning meets the needs of each child, but piques their curiosity without placing too much emphasis on getting the right answer. Instead, the focus is on finding a solution that is innovative, creative, and adaptable to a variety of situations and contexts. The learning is ongoing, as it connects each learner to the world outside the classroom in an authentic context.	**Creativity** **Collaboration** **Critical Thinking** **Communication**	Personalizes learning to meet the needs of each child by adapting to each situation presented, as determined by continuous formative assessment. The planning focus is on the development of open-ended challenges that meet each child where they are and guide them to grow as creative and flexible learners. A consistent effort to question and plan based on the responses given develops into an adaptable approach to teaching.

> **Take Note**: It is important to teach and assess all twenty-first-century skills in the context of every project. This encourages us to see progression, over time, of our learners' skill development. As we chart this growth, we are better prepared to adapt our lesson and scaffolding approach to make it more personalized for the needs of our kids.

In the first stage, our learners must think critically about the challenge as they identify what they already know and what they need to find out in order to formulate their initial ideas about the purpose of the challenge and the final product they have been asked to complete. As our learners individually rely on personal experiences and knowledge, they collaboratively and collectively intersect those ideas with the authentic challenge. They identify the connections between their own experiences, the experiences of their teammates, and the knowledge the challenge requires. What learners discover in Stage 1 is shared, used collaboratively, analyzed, and applied to create something tangible as they progress toward finding a solution. As we intentionally make space for each of our twenty-first-century skills, at every stage, we ensure individual and team creativity is at the forefront of everything our learners do in their quest to find a solution. Their own work and thinking, as outlandish and nonsensical as it may seem in the beginning, is theirs. This makes it a personal learning journey for each of our kids. Thus, our learners maintain engagement and motivation throughout the duration of a project when they are focused on work that is authentic and personal to them.

Our children build on their personal motivations through the use of their own work. This counters the complaint we often hear from teachers: a lack of buy-in from their kids. As we think back to the first stage of Finding a Solution, there are a few questions to ponder. Did we encourage enough ownership as our learners moved from the introduction of a fuzzy problem to defining the problem? Did they create their own questions and begin with their own ideas? Did we introduce the background knowledge to help them represent, in words and diagrams, a concept or relationship? Did our learners write or draw beginning, middle, and end stories and use models to represent the concepts they know? Even if the answers to these questions are affirmative, we typically see many projects end here. Thus, our learners' critical thinking ceases at the application level of design.

Our goal is to design an authentic project-based learning experience that moves our learners beyond the Bloom's application level. Our planning supports our learners' thinking and creativity at each stage, but is not intended to design the solutions for each child or team. As we move to the higher levels of Bloom's Taxonomy, we require our kids to use academic language to support their critical thinking. Their collaboration and communication with one another now becomes more sophisticated, as well. They must think critically to create a solution, because they were moved to dig deeper by our project design. It is our design that takes them through these levels and asks them to demonstrate their thinking and their emotions as they deeply ponder the given challenge. We aid in this undertaking through our encouragement of our learners to use their imagination and abilities to recall, gather, analyze, and compare, before cycling back to their imagination. Thus, the top three levels of Bloom's are necessary to carry out an authentic challenge, as they allow all of our learners to make sense of new vocabulary and to use it in reading, writing, and academic conversations as they solve the given challenge.

In many cases we have already employed the strategies and skills in the lessons we currently design and deliver to bolster natural curiosity through the four Cs. Tables 8.3 to 8.6 align each of the four twenty-first-century skills to the actions that take place during each Stage of Finding a Solution. We have also listed for your reference, in Table 8.2, the verbs that support any scaffolded activities you design.

TABLE 8.2 Planning Verbs

Stages of Finding a Solution	Supports for Planning
Stage 1: Authentic Challenge and Purpose	Use prior knowledge to recall previously learned materials. • match, name, show, tell, answer the five Ws
Stage 2: Information and Prototyping	Demonstrate an understanding of facts and ideas through organization, a statement of the main ideas, interpretation, giving descriptions, and comparisons to apply in a new and different way. • classify, compare, explain, illustrate, summarize, build, model, make use of, plan, utilize
Stage 3: Perspective and Point of View	Examine through identification of motives or causes, make inferences, and find evidence to support their choices. • test for, infer, discover, take part in, divide
Stage 4: Actions and Consequences	Defend options and choices to demonstrate how judgments are made about the impact of their conclusions. • agree, appraise, disprove, rate, interpret, estimate, predict, change
Stage 5: Considerations and Conclusions	Bring information together in a new way to combine new ideas and to create and propose new solutions. • design, create, compose, construct, imagine, invent, make up, develop

Critical Thinking

Our classrooms are delicate ecosystems. The complex network of teacher-to-child and child-to-child interactions has the potential to build up or hold back our kids as learners. The intersection of critical thinking, collaboration, communication, and creativity is where we have the greatest opportunity to foster our learners' natural curiosity through play, exploration, and imagination. Table 8.3 helps us to strategically connect and assess our learners' critical thinking during each stage of the project. This guides us in our alignment of our lessons, activities, assessments, and scaffolds to the type of thinking our learners should do at each stage.

When we begin an authentic project it is necessary to ensure our learners understand the project and its purpose. If they don't, we risk the chance that they will engage in faulty thinking or determine inaccurate results due to a lack of clarity on the purpose of and desired product for the project. Here we want them to connect any personal

TABLE 8.3 Critical Thinking

Stages of Finding a Solution	Critical Thinking
Stage 1: Authentic Challenge and Purpose	• Relate the project challenge to personal experiences • Ask inquiry-based questions about the challenge • Connect the information they already know to the information they need to discover
Stage 2: Information and Prototyping	• Determine what information is relevant to the challenge and what information they don't need • Identify patterns in the information learned • Troubleshoot prototypes to figure out what is working and what isn't
Stage 3: Perspective and Point of View	• Develop patterns and connections between research, interviews, and peer discussions • Explain why they agree with a certain perspective and disagree with other perspectives • Combine the best points of view to support their solution
Stage 4: Actions and Consequences	• Determine "if … then …" statements • Weigh the positives and negatives of potential consequences related to each action • Use a SCAMPER model to refine their solution
Stage 5: Considerations and Conclusions	• Evaluate the potential impact of their final solution • Consider the possible reactions their audience will have to the final solution • Explain how and why they came to their final conclusion

and relevant experiences they may have to the challenge. This guides their thinking as they develop questions about the challenge and make determinations about what information they will need to investigate in order to successfully complete the challenge. Therefore, our design and planning must incorporate multiple points to embed critical thinking. In fact, critical thinking, at the highest level of Bloom's, requires our learners to produce new content. The project challenge also requires our learners to produce new content. This starts with the first stage of Finding a Solution and is carried throughout the remainder of the project. This is accomplished through reflection prompts, quizzes, journal entries and other tools we already use. The regular incorporation of them into our daily routine provides autonomy and multiple pathways for our learners to demonstrate their critical thinking skills. We also suggest you review the tools in Appendix 1, which we have discussed in more detail in several of the previous chapters, for additional ideas on activities that promote critical thinking.

As our kids sort through and make sense of the information they have gathered, they are required to think critically about that information. They identify what information is germane and what information is not relevant to the project challenge. This information is categorized into patterns as their thinking is shaped and developed as they design their first prototypes of their final product. As Stage 2 progresses, these prototypes are further refined and developed while our learners make tweaks and modifications. The troubleshooting approach further develops their critical thinking skills as they determine what works, what doesn't work, and what works better.

We know our youngest learners live in a world all their own. It is up to us to invert the learning process to expand their world beyond their own thoughts and ideas. This means we shift our teaching approach from an "I do, we do, you do" to a "you do, we do" and if needed, "I do" environment. In Stage 3, the critical thinking requires our children to consider a variety of points of view and calls for our learners to compare, contrast, make judgments, and complete evaluations. To demonstrate mastery, our learners connect the dots between all of the information they gather and begin to synthesize that information garnered from a variety of different sources. Toward the middle of this stage, they have to figure out why they agree with or disagree with certain perspectives. These might include, on the low end, the opinions of their peers and, on a higher level, the opinions of experts with whom they interact. Ultimately, they combine the ideas they choose to formulate their own opinions, as they move into Stage 4.

Young children have the propensity to react, rather than to stop and consider the possible consequences of their actions. In this stage, the mere request that they stop, pause, and consider potential outcomes requires critical thinking. If they take an action, then this conceivable consequence is a very real possibility. Therefore, it is necessary for them to weigh all of the positives and negatives of these potential consequences. Here, the use of a SCAMPER (substitute, combine, adapt, modify, put to another use, eliminate, reverse) model to refine their solution aids in their ability to complete this stage. The SCAMPER model is the very definition of divergent thinking and cannot be completed without the employment of critical thinking.

Once our learners complete the SCAMPER model, either orally for our Pre-K and kindergarten kids or written for our older children, it is time to shift their critical thinking to the final solution. In Stage 5, evaluation literally and figuratively comes into play. Once our kids figure out the implications of their final solution, they are ready to consider the possible reactions of their audience to that final solution. An explanation of how and why they arrived at their final conclusion is required and the practice of this explanation aids our children in their ability to empathize with their audience. In short, they must consider all angles before they finalize their solution to the challenge.

Throughout each stage, it is critical that we create the space to make sure our kids' thinking is transformed into something that is visual to both them, as learners, and us, as teachers. Any way in which their thinking is made visible helps them and us as we assess their critical thinking abilities. This assessment guides our daily planning for our learners as a whole class, in small groups, and for individuals. It also encourages our learners to become aware of their thinking and reflect, not only on content, but on how they think about that content. This refined and developed ability to critically think is the first intersection of a successful approach to an authentic project-based learning experience that fosters natural curiosity.

Collaboration

Successful collaboration comes when a classroom ecosystem is based on trust, consistent routines, and shared procedures. Learners who are empowered to become responsible members of the community and take an ownership of their own actions throughout the day collaborate with others more successfully. Collaborations skills are not inherent, especially when our social and emotional skills are still in their earliest phase. Therefore, our learners need training in collaboration to become adept at the skill, even at the simplest levels. At home, our young learners may not have good collaborative role models and may not be encouraged or given the opportunity to collaborate in ways that transfer the skill in the classroom.

When trust in the classroom is established, in the first stage of the authentic challenge, our children have a platform to comfortably share personal experiences related to the challenge. These personal experiences are the ones they use to link their existing knowledge of the challenge to the information they need to find out about the challenge. Through collaboration, a shared writing activity to create a list of inquiry questions creates a good foundation for the project to move forward in a strategic way. Once that foundation has been set, the space to collaboratively explore project materials develops a common experience that propels the project forward.

TABLE 8.4 Collaboration

Stages of Finding a Solution	Collaboration
Stage 1: Authentic Challenge and Purpose	• Share personal experiences related to the challenge • Use shared writing to create a list of inquiry questions they need to answer during the project • Explore a set of related project materials, in various settings, and together build a common experience
Stage 2: Information and Prototyping	• Combine resources and information gathered • Provide peer feedback on first prototypes • Merge varying pieces of individual prototypes to make a team prototype
Stage 3: Perspective and Point of View	• Develop a visual comparison of peer perspectives • Conduct a discussion activity to share and compare • Combine the best points of view from each group member to create a collaborative outcome
Stage 4: Actions and Consequences	• Ask community experts if their actions will have positive or negative impacts • Role-play their actions and the potential consequences that may result from those actions • Provide an action and have a partner write a possible consequence for that action
Stage 5: Considerations and Conclusions	• Evaluate all the possible solutions that each team member has proposed before finalizing a solution • Participate in the development of the final solution • Collaborative presentations to share the solution with the audience

Within an authentic challenge we are given multiple windows of opportunity to train our kids to improve their collaboration skills at each stage and during every project. We cannot assume our learners have the ability to collaborate in meaningful and effective ways at any age or grade level. Therefore, we cannot invite our learners to collaborate without providing tools and structures that help them achieve their goal.

Let's put ourselves in the shoes of our kids who are just learning how to collaborate. Let's say you and your collaborative team are given ten minutes to brainstorm ideas. You engage in small talk for the first few minutes, a few folks share stories and get comfortable, and then one member of the team calls out that there are only two minutes left to brainstorm. At this point, three people have done all of the talking and two have said nothing. Finally, your team races to brainstorm their ideas and rushes the process. Is this successful collaboration?

What if we instead provided a structure to the brainstorming process to help train our learners on how to collaborate and make choices effectively? We might use an open, narrow, close protocol to lend organization to the brainstorming process. For ten minutes we have our learners go through all phases of the brainstorming process to individually choose their top idea. Based on the developmental ability of our kids, we might choose to time each group or encourage our kids to time themselves. At this open stage, everyone shares their ideas for five minutes. For this, we might share the pen and take notes for our learners, have our learners draw pictures of their ideas, or our learners, on their own, record their team's ideas. Next, for three minutes the team narrows their ideas down to their three choices. Lastly, we close the session for two minutes as we ask the teams to choose their top idea. This open, narrow, close activity has variations and adaptations, but the overall structure helps our teams to effectively collaborate.

Once our learners move into the prototyping stage, it is even more important to facilitate effective collaboration between them. If they haven't already, now is the time to have them combine their resources and the information they gathered in Stage 1. This joint effort helps them to produce an initial prototype that is better than it would be without the shared information, as their knowledge base is expanded through their collective research. Once our kids have individually created a prototype, it is ready for feedback. The first step in receiving feedback is from their peers. This takes the collaborative spirit to another level, but the trust that it is so important to have must also be present for this to be effective. Thus, we want to model the appropriate ways in which effective feedback is given before we set our learners up to engage in a peer feedback session.

We suggest the use of role playing to help prepare them. Additionally, the younger our learners, the smaller the feedback groups we want to create. For our Pre-K kiddos, it is best to partner them and use something as simple as warm and cool feedback. By the time our kids get to third grade they are ready to tackle a feedback protocol such as the Feedback Carousel, developed by the National School Reform Faculty, which is described in Appendix 1. This feedback is taken into consideration as additional prototypes are developed with the end goal of the team proto-type that is a collective of several individual prototype ideas.

Once a collaborative prototype is developed, peer feedback isn't enough. In Stage 4, it is time to turn to available experts. They provide valuable insight into the positive or negative implications of a solution. Thus, it is important that our learners gain the confidence to interact with these adults or, in some cases, older children. In order to facilitate this collaborative approach and to increase their comfort level with the collaborative process, there are several helpful activities we can employ. A role-play situation, in which actions taken and possible consequences are played out, helps our kids to see what could happen in a non-threatening context. Similarly, a simple sharing session in which one child provides the action to which his or her partner writes a possible consequence for that action provides a structured feedback moment. We require a collaborative, rather than an individual approach for both of these activities. In short, the power of two is greater than one and leads to a nearly finished prototype that is almost ready for a public share session.

Our learners need to complete the final stage, together, before the project comes to a close. At this point, each team member has contributed ideas and feedback to the ideas of others. This is the last opportunity to evaluate all possible solutions and solidify any final changes. In this stage, be careful that no one child has taken over the project and forced their solution on their teammates. As long as we have continuously implemented formative assessment checks and monitored our teams, this should not be a problem. Finally, our teams present their collaborative findings to an audience. Relish this moment and take pride in the fact that their combined effort is stronger than the effort of any single learner.

Communication

Authentic challenges provide a positive and nurturing experience for our children, which opens the door for us to foster and model open avenues of communication. Classroom communities that provide these interactions bring learners together through discussion using words and actions that increase each other's level of experience. Each hands-on activity, experience, and opportunity for dialogue builds our learners' abilities to communicate. Our learners express and negotiate ideas at each stage, which provides them with the much-needed repetition to move vocabulary knowledge to conceptual understanding. This authentic and more natural practice of linguistic structures helps our learners to use academic language and build knowledge in a purposeful way.

Communication takes many different forms. The task, age of the child, or the purpose of the project affects the end result of how the learning is articulated. For our youngest learners and emerging writers, drawing is our best option. We know, however, that some of our older kids may do a better job expressing themselves through drawing, so we provide our learners with autonomy and options. Drawings are also used as a supplement to writing. It is important to establish clear lines of communication at the outset of the challenge. From the start, we need to know that our learners understand the challenge and if they do not, we need to determine what is included in their interpretation of the challenge.

Oral articulation, at this stage, is an important form of communication not to be overlooked. Conferencing, small group dialogues, and reciprocal reading are examples of opportunities to engage our learners using oral communication. This stage is the perfect time to implement the I Know/You Know activity from Chapter 5. The protocol provides a structured interaction to help our learners practice their communication skills. The structure gets them up and out of their chairs to share their prototype ideas, the information they have gathered, and their early inferences and predictions. We suggest you use this, or a similar activity, as our children tend to communicate more when in collaborative environments that provide a process for them to follow.

We have already discussed ways in which our learners might begin to ask inquiry questions about the challenge. This is their way of communicating with us what supports they may need us to provide through scaffolded lessons. While we have not specifically asked them what they need, if they ask good questions, they have clearly communicated their needs. This is also the stage in which they articulate a foundational plan for attacking the challenge. What needs to be accomplished and how they intend to do so, lays out a path for them and for us. What they will tackle next and how we will support them now becomes a joint endeavor instead of a one-sided decision.

TABLE 8.5 Communication

Stages of Finding a Solution	Communication
Stage 1: Authentic Challenge and Purpose	• Draw or write their interpretation of what the challenge has asked of them • Ask one or more inquiry questions about the challenge • Articulate a plan of what needs to be accomplished in the challenge
Stage 2: Information and Prototyping	• Compile information needed to answer the inquiry questions developed in Stage 1. • Put into words or drawings the steps taken to develop the prototype • Explain the troubleshooting process and how they fixed a particular part of the prototype
Stage 3: Perspective and Point of View	• Explain the differences between points of view explored • Show the overlap discovered between different points of view • Craft a fictional story that compares different perspectives about their challenge and possible solution
Stage 4: Actions and Consequences	• Ask others what they think might be the results of the implemented solution • Share the consequences of their design and receive feedback on possible changes to make • Discuss the design changes throughout the project and why they were made
Stage 5: Considerations and Conclusions	• Reflect on the project process and the development of their final solution • Use charts, graphs, or diagrams to support their solution • Justify their end solution to their authentic audience

Based on the questions asked at the start of the project, we help to guide our learners as they gather information related to the challenge. In Stage 2, they take the information and start to articulate their answers to the inquiry questions developed in Stage 1. The answers to their questions, formulated through the information they have gathered, provide them with the canvas on which to develop their first prototype. The steps taken to develop this prototype are put into written or spoken words or are drawn. This simple act, alone, speaks volumes on the thought processes of our kids. It provides a formative assessment check, as well as a record of their progress in the project. As they continue in this stage, they make changes to their prototypes. Just as we have them record their thinking behind their first prototype, we must provide the space where they articulate the troubleshooting process and how and why they fixed a particular part of their prototype. If they decided to leave their prototype the same, they must also articulate why they chose not to make any changes to their prototype. Unless our learners have clearly communicated their thinking and the justification behind that thinking, they are not ready to move on to Stage 3.

It is one thing for children to communicate their own ideas and opinions. It is an entirely different skillset for them to communicate the differences between the varieties of the points of view they have explored. The difficulty lies in the fact that they must pull out the differences while they simultaneously determine the overlaps. This merges their ability to think critically and their capacity to communicate those similarities and differences. To take this one step further, the comparisons of different perspectives about the challenge and possible solutions are articulated in the form of a fictional story. This twist on communication intertwines multiple twenty-first-century skills and provides us with an additional formative check for understanding, before our learners move on to Stage 4.

It can be a scary thing for a young child to talk to another person. The fact that we prod our learners to ask for feedback compounds that fear for some children. Thus, we need to support our kids in their journey to ask others what they think might be the results of their solution. Our Pre-K and kindergarten learners may, in fact, not be able to present and communicate their ideas at first. Practice presentations and the inclusion of experts in the middle of the project afford them the time to communicate and present their solutions in a variety of environments. The more often our young learners hold the microphone and share in morning meeting and circle time, the more prepared they are when it is their turn to communicate in front of an expert audience. This is the point at which they also share the consequences of their designs and receive feedback on possible changes. By the end of this stage, our learners need to communicate the changes they have made to their designs throughout the project and explain why those changes were implemented.

Through these clearly communicated Stage 4 changes, our learners demonstrate they are ready to move on to Stage 5 with their final conclusions. While reflection has taken place throughout the project, a more targeted overview of that reflection is appropriate here. Their final solution presentation, whether an oral presentation or a written communication, justifies their ideas to their authentic audience. Here, we encourage the use of charts, graphs, or diagrams to visually support their solution. Summarily, when our learners undoubtedly communicate their solution and the way in which they went about finding that solution, we know, they know, and the audience knows they have achieved success. This success is displayed when our learners present their solutions and confidently represent the skills they have gained, understand the content, and have mastered the standards we set out for them to achieve through the project-based learning experience.

Creativity

Creativity is a skill that is best developed in a supportive and enriched classroom community. Our role is vital as we set the tone for the environmental conditions needed to help our children progress and become aware of their progress, as they seek solutions. We find that adaptable teachers are just as important as adaptable learners as they both engage in the creative process. As we nurture these basic skills, at an early age, and highlight joy and play throughout the process, we guide our young learners to become aware of their risk-taking, notice how their predictions come to fruition, and recognize their steady progression over time.

An example of creativity that propels our users beyond the first and second stage and into the further development of their initial ideas is the Reversal Technique. This technique is a creative process that challenges our learners to improve their products. In Stages 3 and 4, to empower our kids to refine their prototypes, we ask them the exact opposite of the challenge and/or challenge question or ask them to explain their product design in reverse. For the exact opposite approach, we simplify the process by asking our kids to think about how they could cause the problem. From here, we have them brainstorm ideas on how to change behaviors that cause the problem in the first place. This sparks ideas on how to solve the actual challenge and gives us an opportunity to have our kids think outside of the box and employ an empathetic approach to the challenge. The explanation of the reverse of their product design means they start from the end and trace the steps back to the problem. This helps to bring to light any gaps in their design process.

Creativity is the highest level of the revised Bloom's Taxonomy. We, in fact, engage in this level, as we create an authentic project-based learning experience for our learners. The challenge, itself, is written at the level of creativity. Thus, Stage 1 requires our learners to tap into their own creative juices to solve it. However, it is important that our learners first explain why the challenge requires a fresh perspective and a new solution. This is where they ask questions that exhibit out-of-the-box thinking. If one or more of our kids suggest an approach to the challenge that was not an original intent of our design, we get excited, as we know their natural

TABLE 8.6 Creativity

Stages of Finding a Solution	Creativity
Stage 1: Authentic Challenge and Purpose	• Articulate why the challenge needs a fresh perspective and a new solution • Ask questions that exhibit out-of-the-box thinking • Suggest an approach to the challenge that was not an original intent of the teacher's design
Stage 2: Information and Prototyping	• Apply divergent thinking to the challenge • Prototype does not look similar to anything previously designed or developed • Looks at design flaws as opportunities for improvement
Stage 3: Perspective and Point of View	• Take a fresh look at the interviews of experts • View the challenge from multiple points of view • Assimilate dissimilar ideas into the solution for the challenge
Stage 4: Actions and Consequences	• Understand that one answer may not be the only solution • Take the possible negative consequences and turn them into positive possibilities • See the challenge as a process and not just an end solution
Stage 5: Considerations and Conclusions	• Combine seemingly separate ideas into a final solution • Design an innovative solution to the challenge • Develop a presentation that is engaging for your audience

curiosity has been piqued and has pushed them into their creative process. Opportunities for our learners to stretch their imagination and tap into their creativity exist in every facet of the authentic challenge.

Since our challenge is designed to naturally engage our learners' curiosity and creativity, they are eager to move to the second stage of Finding a Solution. With their curiosity piqued, they are ready to dig into as much information as they can find and we can provide. Their questions compound as research, whether through blocks, books, or extended play, and lead them to ask more questions. This is the stage where they have the opportunity to showcase their divergent thinking. We want them to come up with 25 new ways to do something or find 40 new uses for a product. This is where the lines between critical thinking and creativity are easily blurred, as the highest levels of thinking support the delivery of well-designed products. This is why, even at this early stage of prototyping, our kids should not develop prototypes that look similar to anything previously designed or developed. If anything, they look at the composition flaws of other products, and their own, as opportunities to apply their creativity and design for improvement.

Creativity, at its core, is the ability to take a fresh look at a problem, product, or challenge. The same holds true in Stage 3, as we challenge our kids to picture the challenge from multiple points of view. This means they may need to take a different approach to any interviews of experts or, if no experts were involved, the information they gathered about the challenge. They are then ready to assimilate dissimilar ideas and apply them to their solution for the challenge. Thus, they take two or more previously unconnected problem elements and combine them to make something that works.

We have mentioned divergent thinking on several occasions throughout this book. At the heart of divergent thinking, our learners must understand that one answer may not be the only solution. In Stage 4, as our kids consider the potential consequences of their actions, through the creative process, they take the possible negative consequences and figure out how to turn them into positive ones. The reason they can do this is that they see the challenge as a process and not just an end solution. In fact, if we were to come back to the same challenge after several weeks or months away from it, our creative learners would see additional endless possibilities for Finding a Solution.

All creative learners know that simply finding a solution to a challenge isn't enough to convince an audience of its worth. Instead, they also focus on the development of a presentation that is creatively engaging for their audience. In this presentation, they discuss how they combined seemingly separate ideas into a final solution and explain the innovation behind that solution. They creatively communicate their ideas and exhibit an adaptable, flexible, yet interconnected approach to Finding a Solution, as they convince their audience of the plausibility of their conclusions.

As the twenty-first-century skills of our kids are developed, assessed, refined, and mastered, it is important to remember the best learning is adaptable. The authentic project-based learning experience you craft for your kids is established on a few premises:

1   We know our kids bring a diverse array of prior knowledge to our classrooms.
2   It is our responsibility to develop learning experiences that interconnect content with twenty-first-century skills.
3   Our kids learn at varying rates and we must meet them where they are, not where we expect them to be, at any given time.
4   Children are naturally curious and it is up to us to ensure this curiosity blossoms.
5   The adaptability and flexibility of young children is used to our advantage in the classroom, as they create and define things in new ways.

We are glad you took the time to explore deeper ways in which to develop the natural curiosity in your kids. It was a journey for us, as we wrote this book, and we know that you are well into your own journey of developing challenges for your kids. Authentic project-based learning experiences shift the learning for our kids. This approach moves us from a standards-based curriculum for passive learners to a standards-based curriculum for problem-solvers, question-askers, and active participants in their real world. This shift transforms learning for our kids and for us. It connects our schools to our communities. These connections model and reinforce the twenty-first-century skills that lie within every child. We want every child to transform into a successful adult who has the ability to think critically, communicate, collaborate, and be creative. Authentic challenges tap into what is relevant to our children in their present world and what intrinsically motivates them. There is an art to this development of a young generation of problem-solvers. It is our responsibility to maintain their ability to ask "why" over and over again. To connect the bridge between natural curiosity and these twenty-first-century skills that really are innate to all children, we develop authentic project-based learning experiences for them to explore.

Where are You?
What are You Thinking?
How do You Feel?

Take Action	Seek Community	Think Aloud
Choose two or three of your favorite chapters or parts of this book. Critically reflect on them and how they impact you personally. What are you naturally curious about? What motivates you to dig deeper? As you move forward, what challenges do you want to take on now and in the future, with whom do you want to collaborate, and what will you create within and beyond your classroom community?	Communicate your ideas for the future with a teaching partner and challenge them to join you. Collaborate with a partner on a new idea that you would like to develop into an authentic challenge. How can you inspire creativity and motivate each other?	After reading this chapter, and the entirety of this book, what adjustments have you made in your thought processes about the impact of incorporating an authentic project-based learning experience that involves all aspects of our twenty-first-century skill set? What ideas do you have for your own authentic challenge that you are ready to start planning?

Appendix 1

A Guide to Tools, Activities, and Protocols

All of the tools, activities, and protocols shared here are designed to work with any age and any grade level. Make adjustments as needed and as appropriate for your learners. In many of the chapters, we have provided you with ideas for modifications. This is meant to be a quick reference guide for your planning purposes.

3-2-1 Reflection

- Exit ticket reflection strategy
- List three things learned
- List two things found interesting
- List one question you still have

3-12-3 Brainstorm

- Three minutes to brainstorm general ideas about the topic—individuals in the group write ideas on index cards
- Twelve minutes to combine ideas into a rough concept—pair off and draw three index cards to shape thinking
- Three minutes to share rough concept with the group

Agreement Circles

- Arrange children in a circle
- Provide a statement for the class to consider
- All learners who agree with the statement move to the center of the circle
- Match children up to form pairs between an agreer and a non-agreer
- Discuss for a few minutes
- Share out as a class

Anchor Charts

- Anchor charts make thinking and processes visible
- As you uncover new strategies, processes, cues, guidelines, and other content create a chart to visually represent the learning

Author Study

- An author study is a lesson that gives learners the opportunity to delve deeply into an author's life and body of work. Critically evaluate an author's themes, characters, and writing style.

Be the Illustrator

- Use a wordless book or make your own book without text.
- Ask learners to come up with captions for each picture that tells a story.
- Have them tell you what is happening in each picture while you record their words under each picture.
- Then read the story as they have written it.

Café Conversations (The World Café)

- Small group conversations with question stems
- Three rounds lasting 5 to 7 minutes each
- Paper to write, doodle, and draw in each group
- Table host stays while others travel to new conversations with new ideas, themes, and questions

Circle Square Triangle Reflection

- ◆ Exit ticket reflection strategy
- ◆ Draw a triangle and list three important points from the day or the reading
- ◆ Draw a square and write down anything that they agree or are "square" with
- ◆ Draw a circle and write down any question they might still have or is "circling" in their mind
- ◆ Note: This is a good opportunity to talk about "being square" with a concept and having a question that is "circling" in their mind.

Cognitive Content Dictionary (GLAD)

- ◆ Teacher chooses a vocabulary word for the week
- ◆ Predict the meaning of the word
- ◆ Write or sketch something that helps them remember the word
- ◆ Use the word in a sentence
- ◆ Can be done individually, in small groups, or as a whole class

Comparative Input Chart (GLAD)

- ◆ Choose two objects to compare
- ◆ Use pictures to make the comparisons
- ◆ Add words to the comparisons
- ◆ Create a Venn diagram as a visual representation of the comparisons

Consequence and Sequel

- ◆ Based on the premise that a new invention, plan, rule, or decision has consequences that go on for a long time
- ◆ Learners consider the immediate, short-term, medium-term, and long-term consequences of an action (make time adaptations as appropriate for young children, as they can't focus as far into the future)
- ◆ Others often see the consequences of your solution when you do not

Conversation Station (Balanced Literacy Diet)

- ◆ Create a reusable sign that reads: "Let's talk about ——."
- ◆ Set up the table and chairs

◆ Gather props, make vocabulary card, and gather related books
◆ Find a storybook that models conversational practices (We like *Mice Squeak, We Speak* by Arnold Shapiro)

Co-op Strip Paragraphs (GLAD)

◆ Provide a topic sentence—GLAD uses one created via the Process Grid activity
◆ Every child or every group is responsible for adding a sentence to the original
◆ The class reads the co-created paragraph, together

Experts in the House

◆ Create an expert group based on the Process Grid
◆ Much like a jigsaw method, chose one learner from each group to represent a concept
◆ Expert groups research information
◆ Expert groups share information with the class or with their original groups

Feedback Carousel (National School Reform Faculty)

◆ Display the main components of your idea on a piece of chart paper and hang on a wall or lay on a table
◆ Divide a second sheet of chart paper into four quadrants: clarifying questions, probing questions, recommendations, and resources
◆ Learners walk around the room and provide feedback
◆ Sticky notes are used to place the feedback in the appropriate quadrant

Frayer Model/Four Box Vocabulary

◆ Create a diagram that is similar to the Reframing Matrix
◆ Use the center of the diagram to list the vocabulary word
◆ Use each of the four segmented portions of the rectangle to list each of the following:

— Definition
— Examples
— Non-examples
— Illustration of the vocabulary word

GRASPS

- ◆ Identify the real-world connection to each of the following:
    - — Goal
    - — Role
    - — Audience
    - — Situation
    - — Product/Performance
    - — Standards

Guided Reciprocal Teaching or Peer Teaching

- ◆ Learners take on the roles and lead their own discussions
- ◆ Roles to include:
    - — Questioning
    - — Clarifying
    - — Summarizing
    - — Predicting

I Know/You Know (Literacy TA)

- ◆ Structured Pair Share
- ◆ Partner A shares for 30 seconds. Partner B actively listens, takes notes
- ◆ Partner B summarizes what Partner A shared for 30 seconds
- ◆ Partner A shares for 30 seconds. Partner B actively listens, takes notes
- ◆ Partner B summarizes what Partner A shared for 30 seconds
- ◆ Find new partners, repeat four times

Inside Outside Circles (Kagan)

- ◆ Form two circles of kids with one circle literally inside of the other
- ◆ Partner learners with one from the inside circle and the other from the outside circle
- ◆ Partner A summarizes the information from the story or lesson (timed)
- ◆ Partner B listens and then adds to the summary (timed)
- ◆ Move the outside circle round by two people
- ◆ New partners repeat the process
- ◆ The teacher listens from the center of the two circles

Interactive Journal

- ◆ Graphically Organized Reading Notes
- ◆ Encourage developmentally appropriate independent writing

Knowledge Inventories

- ◆ Determine what prior knowledge exists with an individual child
- ◆ Learners take turns and orally share prior knowledge or gained knowledge
- ◆ Small groups or partners write down key words or phrases

Knowledge Tree Guides

- ◆ Learners collaboratively "grow a tree" about information in an activity or experience
- ◆ The three branches of the tree include:
  - – A glossary of terms
  - – One comment and one question from an assigned reading
  - – One response to another's question or a comment

Mentor Text

- ◆ Show kids good writing
- ◆ Deconstruct the writing

Mind Maps

- ◆ Represent the main idea through an image or chosen word
- ◆ Create branches to represent pictures or words related to the main idea
- ◆ Connect additional sub-branches that extend ideas and thinking

Narrative Input Chart (GLAD)

- ◆ Choose a story or adapt a story to include academic language and vocabulary from the unit
- ◆ Find pictures that relate to the parts of the story and attach the related narrative section to the back of the appropriate picture
- ◆ Tell the narrative through the pictures
- ◆ Revisit the narrative and add speech bubbles or words

Observation Chart (GLAD)

- ◆ Provide color photos of the topic on poster paper
- ◆ Groups of learners are given one marker only and, as a group, write
  - − An observation
  - − A question
  - − A comment

Open-Narrow-Close

- ◆ Open Phase: Generate as many ideas as possible
- ◆ Narrow Phase: Clarify, categorize, and prioritize possible solutions
- ◆ Close Phase: Select a final solution to implement

Pass Around Strategy

- ◆ Learners work in cooperative writing groups to develop a variety of possible stories around a single prompt.

Process Grid (GLAD)

- ◆ Categorize concepts from the project
- ◆ Use the concepts and the categories to create a grid
- ◆ Learners collaboratively fill in the grid with important information

Pyramid Teaching

- ◆ Keep a record of ideas and solutions
- ◆ Create a process for kids to follow to chart their ideas and solutions through either writing or drawing
- ◆ Schedule discussions with small groups or individual kids
- ◆ Make reflective changes throughout the project
- ◆ Require them to make justifications for changes made

Quiz-Quiz-Trade

- ◆ Peer review of information by asking and answering questions to think about solutions
- ◆ Learners are given a question to solve and then they find a partner to quiz and vice versa
- ◆ Once finished, they break off and find new partners

Reflective Central Idea Diagram

- Central or main idea in the center with lines radiating from center
- Each lines connects to new box
- Each box contains a question: Where did we start? Where are we now? Where are we going?
- Reflective diagramming assists a learner in synthesizing information based on investigations and designs

Reframing Matrix

- Create a four-box grid with the problem or challenge listed in the center
- Use the 4Ps to fill in the boxes with the following perspectives:
  - People
  - Product
  - Planning
  - Potential

Reversal Technique

- Identify the problem or challenge
- Reverse the problem—"How could I possibly cause the problem?"
- Brainstorm to generate reverse solution ideas
- Evaluate these solution ideas and how they help to see the original problem in a new light

Roving Reporter

- One team member moves around the room to gather information
- Report back to their team any ideas that might be useful

SCAMPER

- A mnemonic that stands for substitute, combine, adapt, modify, put to another use, eliminate, and reverse
- Use the words to create specific questions as solutions to challenges are considered

Scan for Vocabulary Tool

- ◆ Read and list all of the unfamiliar words
- ◆ Create a personal glossary of terms that includes synonyms and examples

See Think Wonder

- ◆ Answer the following questions
  - – What do you see?
  - – What do you think about what you see?
  - – What do you wonder about what you see?

Socratic Seminar

- ◆ Arrange kids in a circle
- ◆ Ask a guiding question for the discussion
- ◆ Have kids respond to the question in a discussion format, but encourage them to ask questions during the discussion
- ◆ Every time someone asks a question, clap your hands and record the question
- ◆ At the conclusion of the discussion, affinity map the questions
  - – Have your learners determine three categories for the questions
  - – Categorize the questions into the categories
  - – Use the categories of questions to take the next steps in the project
- ◆ Note: This is our version of this popular discussion approach

Space Method

- ◆ *Summary*: Today I learned … The main idea(s) …
- ◆ *Process*: As I recorded information, I thought about … I was challenged today because …
- ◆ *Analyze*: —— (topic) consist of … X and Y are critical concepts …
- ◆ *Connect*: While learning about ——, I thought of … Topic X is similar to …
- ◆ *Evaluate*: Today was helpful because … It's important to understand …

Spider Web Discussion

- ◆ Place kids in a circle
- ◆ Provide a discussion prompt or question

- ◆ Use chart paper to identify where kids sit in the circle
- ◆ As kids participate in the discussion, map the conversation by drawing lines between each child as they talk
- ◆ The end result should look like a spider web
- ◆ This is loosely based on the Harkness Discussion Protocol with a few modifications
- ◆ We like to give bonus participation to our kids who take the conversation to the next level by asking a deep question or appropriately challenging a comment made by a peer
- ◆ For much older learners, we do this as a pass/fail activity— everyone must participate to pass or everyone fails
- ◆ Children learn communication skills as they figure out how to skillfully draw individuals into a conversation

Start, Stop, Continue

- ◆ Team reflection process
- ◆ Individuals determine and share out the following:
  - – What they want to start doing
  - – What they want to stop doing
  - – What they want to continue doing

Story Maps

- ◆ Use a story that has a clear problem and a defined outcome
- ◆ List the problem, the characters, the events that took place leading up to the solution, and the final solution

SWOT Analysis (Good, Grow, Possible, Buggy)

- ◆ What are the strengths, weaknesses, opportunities, and threats to a possible solution?
- ◆ Look at these from both an internal and external frame of reference (things we can control and things we can't)

Team Tasks (GLAD)

- ◆ Use in lieu of centers
- ◆ Teacher models a task (any task)
- ◆ Teams work together on the task
- ◆ Task is given to an individual to complete

Text Clue Conclusion Groups

- ◆ Read a text
- ◆ Identify personal connections to the text
- ◆ Learners map or the teacher maps personal connections
- ◆ Look for patterns
- ◆ Connect patterns to a challenge or issue

Think it Through

- ◆ Role-play real-life scenarios
- ◆ Use cause and effect to discuss consequences and that consequences affect others

Three-Step Interview

- ◆ Work in pairs to interview each other (steps one and two)
- ◆ Take turns sharing information to the entire group (step three)

To Be or Not to Be Protocol

- ◆ Peer partners share the biggest problem encountered with the identified solution
- ◆ Feedback
- ◆ Reflection

Upside Down Gallery Walk

- ◆ Teams or individual learners display their work on a large poster
- ◆ Teams or individual learners analyze posters and provide feedback on a sticky note
- ◆ All feedback is written on the sticky side and then the sticky note is placed on the poster so that no one is able to read the feedback until the end of the walk

Yarn–Yarn

- ◆ The structure provides a record of interaction patterns
- ◆ Each time a team member wants to talk, he/she must wrap the yarn around his/her finger
- ◆ At the end of the conversation, the visual should provide information for reflection on who did the most/least amount of talking

Appendix 2
Templates and Tools

The following pages are templates and tools to help you think through the planning process and create standards-based scaffolding for your learners.

Use this table to help you plan your authentic learning experience. Jot down notes, ideas, and possible activities to include in your challenge design.

Stages of Finding a Solution	
Stage 1	
Authentic Challenge and Purpose	
How do we know if our kids understand the challenge and why they are doing it?	
Stage 2	
Information and Prototyping	
How do we know if our kids have created a viable prototype?	
Stage 3	
Perspective and Point of View	
How do we know if our kids have thought about different ideas?	
Stage 4	
Actions and Consequences	
How do we know if our kids have moved beyond their initial beliefs?	
Stage 5	
Considerations and Conclusions	
How do we know if our kids have reached the best possible solution for their audience?	

Bloom's Taxonomy - Scaffold Your Questions for the Authentic Challenge

CREATE -

EVALUATE

ANALYZE

APPLY

UNDERSTAND

REMEMBER

Stages of Finding a Solution

Stage 5
Considerations and Conclusions
How do we know if our kids have reached the best possible solution for their audience?

Stage 4
Actions and Consequences
How do we know if our kids have moved beyond their initial beliefs?

Stage 3
Perspective and Point of View
How do we know if our kids have thought about different ideas?

Stage 2
Information and Prototyping
How do we know if our kids have created a viable prototype?

Stage 1
Authentic Challenge and Purpose
How do we know if our kids understand the challenge and why they are doing it?

Bloom's Taxonomy - Scaffold Your Questions for the Authentic Challenge

CREATE -

EVALUATE

ANALYZE

APPLY

UNDERSTAND

REMEMBER

Appendix 3

Possible Challenge Questions for the Community-Based Project Ideas in Table 1.4

Community Attraction	Project Idea
Theatre	Write a community-based play • How can we write a play that reflects our community? Create a marionette performance • How can we create a marionette performance that represents an important issue to us?
Park	Sponsor a park conservation event • How can we best conserve our park? Design a plan to make children more active by using the park in new ways • How can we design a plan to get our friends to use the park more often?
Food Bank	Develop kid-generated cookbooks and painted fabric grocery bags to give away at the food bank • How can we write a cookbook that people will want to buy? Senior Box Letters—develop a pen pal program with seniors citizens who receive box lunches from the local food banks • How can we make senior citizens feel loved when they receive their lunches from the food bank or Meals on Wheels?

Zoo	Create a campaign to improve the viewing spaces outside of the animal habitats from a 3–4 foot perspective
	• How can we improve the viewing areas at the zoo for visitors of all heights?
	Offer a redesign of various exhibits to make them more child friendly
	• How can we redesign an exhibit at the zoo to make it better for our friends?
Botanical Gardens	Design an interactive exhibit where young visitors can play to learn about the parts of a plant
	• How can we design an interactive exhibit that kids will want to see and can learn from?
	Create a walking tour, as they learn about the life cycles of plants and insects, that highlights the best photographic spaces for families with little kids
	• How can we plan the best walking tour to help kids learn about the life cycle of plants and insects?
Fire House	Design a persuasive video to convince your family why you need a survival kit and develop the emergency evacuation plan for your home
	• How do we create a survival kit campaign for our parents and caregivers?
	Plan a natural disaster assembly at your school to help to update the school's emergency plans
	• How do we update our school's emergency evacuation plans so that we are as safe as possible?
Animal Shelter	Partner with a local shelter to devise a plan to increase the number of animals adopted.
	• How can we get more people to adopt pets instead of buying pets?
	Design a plan to help reduce the number of animals dropped off at the shelter
	• How can we reduce the number of unwanted animals dropped off at our local animal shelter?
Library	Develop a mini-lending library house for the neighborhood
	• How can we design a mini-lending library for our neighborhood?
	Plan an "open-mic" night for original short story readings
	• How can we write an original short story that is good enough to be read at an open-mic night at the library?

Select Bibliography

3-12-3 Brainstorm (n.d.). Gamestorming. Retrieved from http://gamestorming. com/games-for-design/3-12-3-brainstorm/.

Beaty, A. (2007). *Iggy Peck architect*. New York: Abrams Books for Young Readers.

Becker, K. (2013). *My dream playground*. Somerville, MA: Candlewick.

Blackledge, A. (2005). *Small pet care: How to look after your rabbit, guinea pig, or hamster*. New York: DK Publishing.

Boehm, A. (2001). *Jack in search of art*. Lanham, MD: Rhinehart, Roberts.

Boushey, G., and Moser J. (2006). *The daily 5: Fostering literacy independence in the elementary grades*. Portland, ME: Stenhouse.

Bowkett, S. (2013). *Archidoodle: The architect's activity book*. London: Laurence King.

Children's Internet Protection Act (n.d.). Federal Communications Commission. Retrieved from https://www.fcc.gov/consumers/guides/childrens-internet-protection-act.

Children's Online Privacy Protection Act (n.d.). Federal Trade Commission. Retrieved from https://www.ftc.gov/enforcement/rules/rulemaking-regulatory-reform-proceedings/childrens-online-privacy-protection-rule.

Consequence and Sequel (n.d.). Cort Learning. Retrieved from http://www.cortthinking.net/files/student-pdfs/CoRT1/CoRT1_4.pdf.

Cummins, J. (2002). *County kid, city kid*. New York: Henry Holt.

Dalton, J., and Smith, D. (1986). *Extending children's special abilities: Strategies for primary classrooms*. Melbourne, Vic.: Curriculum Branch, Schools Division.

Daywalt, D. (2013). *The day the crayons quit*. New York: Philomel Books.

Family Educational Rights and Privacy Act (n.d.). United States Department of Education. Retrieved from http://www2.ed.gov/policy/gen/guid/fpco/ferpa/index.html.

Feedback Carousel (n.d.). National School Reform Faculty. Retrieved from http://www.nsrfharmony.org/system/files/protocols/feed_back_carousel.pdf.

Forward, T. (2005). *The wolf's story*. Somerville, MA: Candlewick.

Grey, M. (2004). *The pea and the princess*. London: Red Fox.

Guay, F., Vallerand, R.J., and Blanchard, C. (2000). On the assessment of situational intrinsic and extrinsic motivation: The Situational Motivation Scale (SIMS). *Motivation and Emotion*, 24, 3, 175–213. Retrieved from https://selfdeterminationtheory.org/SDT/documents/2000_Guay VallerandBlanchard_MO.pdf.

Hall, D. (1994). *I am the dog, I am the cat*. New York: Dial Books.

Hooks, W.H. (1996). *Mr. Garbage*. New York: Byron Preiss Visual Publications.

Hopkinson, D. (1997). *Sweet Clara and the freedom quilt*. New York: Alfred A. Kopf.

Inside Outside Circles (n.d.). Kagan Strategies. Retrieved from https://wvde.state.wv.us/strategybank/Inside-OutsideCircle.html.

Johnston, T. (1996). *The quilt story*. New York: Penguin Putnam Books for Young Readers.

Knowles, M., Holton, E., and Swanson, R. (2005). *The adult learner: The definitive classic in adult education and human resource development* (6th ed.). Burlington, MA: Butterworth-Heinemann.

Laur, D. (2013). *Authentic learning experiences: A real-world approach to project-based learning.* London: Routledge.

Look, L. (2013). *Brush of the gods.* New York: Random Schwartz and Wade.

Macaulay, D. (2010). *Built to last.* Boston, MA: HMH Books for Young Readers.

McNamara, M., and Gordon, M. (2004). *The playground problem.* New York: Scholastic.

Manushkin, F. (2011). *Katie and the class pet.* Mankato, MN: Picture Window Books.

Müller, F., and Louw, J. (2004). Learning environment, motivation and interest: Perspectives on self-determination theory. *South African Journal of Psychology,* 34, 2, 169–190.

National Governor's Association for Best Practices, Council of Chief State Officers (2010). Common Core State Standards Initiative. Washington, D.C.: National Governor's Association for Best Practices, Council of Chief State Officers.

NGSS Lead States (2013). *Next Generation Science Standards: For states, by states.* Washington, D.C.: The National Academies Press.

Osborne, M. (1992–). "Magic Tree House" series. New York: Random House Books for Young Readers.

Partnership for 21st Century Learning at http://www.p21.org.

Pennsylvania Learning Standards for Early Childhood (n.d.). Office of Childhood Development and Early Learning. Retrieved from https://www.pakeys.org/uploadedContent/Docs/Career%20Development/2014%20Pennsylvania%20Learning%20Standards%20for%20Early%20Childhood%20PreKindergarten.pdf.

Prensky, M. (2001). Digital natives, digital immigrants. Retrieved from http://www.marcprensky.com/writing/Prensky%20-%20Digital%20Natives,%20Digital%20Immigrants%20-%20Part1.pdf.

Principles of Content-Based Instruction (n.d.). Center for Advanced Research on Language Acquisition. Retrieved from http://carla.umn.edu/cobaltt/modules/principles/index.html.

Project GLAD (n.d.). Orange County Department of Education. Retrieved from http://projectgladstudy.educationnorthwest.org/what-is-glad.

Responsive Classroom (n.d.). Responsive Classroom. Retrieved from https://www.responsiveclassroom.org.

Roy, R. (1997–). "A to Z mysteries" series. New York: Penguin Random House.

SCAMPER (n.d.). MindTools. Retrieved from https://www.mindtools.com/pages/article/newCT_02.htm.

Scieszka, J. (1989). *The true story of the three little pigs.* New York: Viking Press.

Seuss, D. (1971). *The lorax.* New York: Random House Books for Young Readers.

Shapiro, A. (2000). *Mice squeak, we speak.* New York: Puffin Books.

Storad, C. (2014). *Gator, gator second grader: Classroom pet or not?* Chandler, AZ: Little Five Star.

Stringer, L. (2013). *When Stravinsky met Nijinsky: Two artists, their ballet, and one extraordinary riot.* San Diego, CA: Harcourt.

Three-Step Interview Process (n.d.). Kagan. Retrieved from http://et.nwresd.org/files/Three_Step_Interview.pdf.

Van Allsburg, C. (1990). *Just a dream*. Boston, MA: Houghton Mifflin.

Viva, F. (2013). *Young Frank, architect*. New York: Harry N. Abrams.

Wiggins, G., and McTighe, J. (2004). *Understanding by design professional development workbook*. Alexandria, VA: Association for Supervision and Curriculum Development.

Winter, J. (2013). *Henri's scissors*. New York: Simon & Schuster.